FLIGHTS INTO
BIBLICAL
ARCHAEOLOGY

FLIGHTS INTO BIBLICAL ARCHAEOLOGY

Photography: Duby Tal
Piloting: Moni Haramati
Text: Prof. Shimon Gibson

Planning & Editing: Duby Tal and Prof. Shimon Gibson
Scientific advisor: Dr Sam Wolff, IAA
Graphic Design: Studio Ze

Scanning: Nati Cohen, Shahaf Nagar, Adi Digmi
Editing Co–ordinator: Meyrav Blankleder

Printing and Binding: Lion production Ltd.
Production: Albatross Aerial Photography Ltd.

Additional Photography:
- Page 59, bottom: Prof. Ephraim Stern, Tel Dor Project, Hebrew University, Jerusalem.
- Page 96, bottom, and page 141, bottom: Shmuel Magal
- Page 101, top left: Dr Yitzhak Magen, Staff Officer of Archaeology Civil Administration of Judea and Samaria, IAA.
- Page 118, middle right: Dr. Danny Syon, IAA, Acre
- Page 120, top, middle, left: Karim Abu Mokh, Shuni Archaeological Project, Jewish National Fund.
- Page 167, bottom: Yotam Tepper. Excavations of the Megiddo Prison 2005. IAA Jerusalem.

First edition, printed in Israel, 2007
Second edition, printed in Israel, 2008
Third edition, printed in China, 2010

ISBN 978-965-90283-4-4
Danakod 531-8

This book was published in association with the Israel Antiquities Authority, POB 586, Jerusalem 91004, Israel.

ALBATROSS

skyline@albatross.co.il
11 Wingate st. Herzlia 46643, ISRAEL
Tel: +972-9-9540066 Fax: +972-9-9540088
www.albatross.co.il

FLIGHTS INTO BIBLICAL ARCHAEOLOGY

Duby Tal – Photography

Moni Haramati – Piloting

Shimon Gibson – Text

ALBATROSS

ISRAEL ANTIQUITIES AUTHORITY רשות העתיקות

Contents

Part Five:
ISLAM AND THE CRUSADERS 194

Part Six:
TOWARDS MODERN TIMES 238

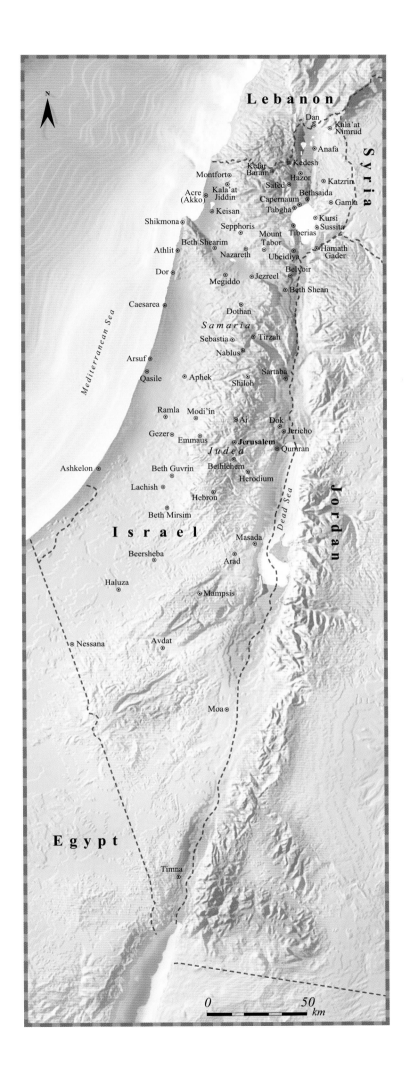

Preface

Duby Tal

History and Archaeology were my constant childhood companions, first as a youngster listening to my mother's riveting stories of her travels at the time of the Second World War with the British Army to far–flung places such as the ruins of Baalbek in Lebanon and the Pyramids in Egypt, and then, when I participated in the many trips that my mother organized throughout the Land of Israel.

Later, as a young helicopter pilot, I became enthralled by the different angles of perception that flight allowed me to obtain. Flying low in my craft, I was fascinated by the signs and symbols of antiquity that would flash through thick undergrowth or cast weird shadows across the desert sands.

Since I knew many of these sites from the ground, I realized there were many things that one could see from the air that it was impossible to see from the ground. As a result, it wasn't long before I was also adding a love of photography to my passion for flying, and thus I began a life–long career as a landscape photographer, specializing in oblique aerial views of the countryside.

When one is flying low in the skies, a highly intimate relationship is formed with the surface of the land that is below you. It has been my privilege to be born in a land of such great antiquity, where each stone has an amazing story, where almost every place seems to have been the focus of an ancient saga.

Whispering tales of early man emerge from the rolling hills and deep valleys, and sandy coasts of the land which we all know and love as modern Israel. Its archaeological features resound with memories of the Old and New Testaments, and of a multitude of peoples, who lived here or tramped through it, including the Greeks and Romans, Jews and Christians, Arabs and Crusaders. So many people passed through this land before seemingly disappearing, but their memory is still retained by the archaeological sites.

For thirty years I have flown these skies, as a pilot and then as an aerial photographer, together with my highly gifted partner in the skies, Moni Haramati. Throughout this time I have never ever tired of watching the ever–changing march of time unfolding in the lands beneath me.

I am filled with renewed wonder each time I am able to observe the sites, even the well known ones, drenched by the golden rays of the setting sun in the summer, or covered by a fresh mantle of snow in the blue light of an early winter's morning. Time and time again I return high up in the sky and begin chasing once again the light and the individual essence of each place within the magnificence of its setting.

I never tire of the excitement when a seemingly–unexplored place is suddenly revealed to me for the first time. The thrill of discovery from the air is something I believe I share with the archaeologists themselves who are working on the ground. However, I should also mention the credit that I believe is due to the archaeologists for their hard work and daily toil, something that commands both our respect and support. Without them many of these sites would simply be heaps in the ground.

Ancient remains are an integral part of the overall landscape, with layers of history superimposed one upon the other. Indeed, archaeology is the thread that connects and combines history, with physical geography, into one interdisciplinary story. Archaeologist Professor Shimon Gibson has shared my passion for this book and has provided richly informed texts which I hope will bring the multi–faceted tapestry of the ancient past of this country to life.

I hope that this book succeeds in conveying to you some of the richness and variety in the ancient landscapes of the Land of Israel.

Tell Rekesh: a perfect ancient mound (tell) in the Lower Galilee with the remains of superimposed ancient cities which have never been tested by the spade. Surface indications date from the Bronze and Iron Ages.

Introduction

Professor Shimon Gibson

The search for the ancient past of the Land of Israel is an exciting process and new discoveries are made all the time. Excavation is the principal method used by archaeologists in the search for information about ancient cultures, but it is not just about digging holes in the ground. Indeed, excavations are conducted nowadays using rigorous scientific techniques. The American archaeologist William Foxwell Albright once wrote that "excavation is both art and science" and the British archaeologist Mortimer Wheeler remarked that "there is no correct method of excavation, but many wrong ones."

The nineteenth century was a period of incipient exploration and treasure hunting. The early twentieth century saw the wide–scale excavation of ancient mounds (tells) with the attempt to dig down to levels with biblical associations as quickly as possible. During the course of the twentieth century scientific techniques of excavation improved considerably, with sensitive area–excavations of a more limited and solid scientific nature being conducted, and with refined material studies of ceramic and environmental remains being initiated. This was the peak of "Biblical Archaeology" with the general public fascinated with the spectacular discoveries at Dan, Hazor, Lachish and Beersheba, as well as with sites of later date such as at Masada, and since the 1970s, in Jerusalem, with excavations close to the Temple Mount and in the Jewish Quarter.

In recent decades, archaeology in the Holy Land has become a much more scientific discipline with the flourishing of procedures such as calibrated radiocarbon and thorium–uranium methods of dating, and with anthropological, DNA and zoological and botanical techniques being adapted for the investigation of materials derived from excavations. Aerial photography is also utilized for research, with the study of pictures taken from aircraft or balloons. Many areas of specialization have developed in the field of archaeology, not only in terms of the various ancient periods studied, but also in terms of the interest in specific groups of artifacts (e.g. weapons, stamped seals, beads, glass objects, and so forth). Pottery studies are so well developed nowadays that some experts can date ceramic vessels of certain periods to within a fifty–year time span.

The Israel Antiquities Authority, founded in 1989 (a successor to the Israel Department of Antiquities and Museums) , is the official governmental regulatory power for all archaeological activities conducted in Israel: inspecting known sites with antiquities and ensuring their protection, fighting illegal excavations and regulating the trade in antiquities, and issuing licenses for archaeological excavation projects. It also conducts numerous salvage digging operations prior to modern housing and road development schemes.

Human beings have always yearned to grasp things visual, whether of buildings or houses, monuments, landscapes, manifestations of nature, animals, public events and, of course,

Chronological Chart

Palaeolithic	Epipalaeolithic	Neolithic	Chalcolithic	Early Bronze Age	Intermediate Bronze Age	Middle Bronze Age	Late Bronze Age	Iron Age	Babylonian/ Persian
1,400.000-17,000	17,000-8500	8500-4500	4500-3500	3500-2350	2350-2000	2000-1550	1550-1200	1200-586	586-332
Before Present	B.C.E	B.C.E	B.C.E	B.C.E	B.C.E	B.C.E	B.C.E	B.C.E	B.C.E

our fellow human beings (usually family members), and nowadays, with the aid of the fast–developing technology of digital photography, everyone can do so. But, at the same time, the internet and television are drowning us in pictorial imagery and we can get whatever we want, all the time. As a result, we look around ourselves and see things, and yet we do not really see the things we want to, our eyes glossing over everyday imagery, and perhaps this is because our brains are over–compensating and extrapolating, allowing us to fill in the gaps, to see what is not necessarily there. Hence, I can identify a desire within myself and within others, to see the same recognizable features but from a totally different perspective, from high up in the sky.

In ancient times viewing landscapes and places of abode from up high, was largely regarded as the privilege of the gods. Shrines and temples were built on the summits of the highest mountains available, and the Bible tells us that Moses climbed to the top of Mount Sinai, communicated with God and thus received the Tablets of the Law. People in early times tried to imagine various aspects of the holy floating and hovering in the sky like clouds or flying and soaring, at will and majestically, like birds. Daedalus, according to legend, tried to reach even further; his son Icarus flew too close to the sun and then fell out of the sky, spiraling down to his death. Hence, it was God or the gods who were perceived by human beings in antiquity as the supreme owners of the sky. We may therefore feel lucky – living in the age of the

invention of aircraft – that we too can enter the holy domain of the sky, and view the archaeological sites and landscapes of the Holy Land, but free from the inhibitions of ancient times. Aerial photographs – vertical shots taken from light aircraft, balloons and oblique views from helicopters – allow one to view archaeological sites as cohesive and overall entities. The first aerial shots of the Holy Land were taken during the First World War and their usefulness for historical geography and exploration was quickly realized by scholars. Since then oblique shots of archaeological sites have been regularly made throughout the land, recording facets of landscapes which have now disappeared as a result of the sheer scale of modern development.

Duby Tal, with Moni Haramati's piloting skills, has taken pictures of archaeological sites that are not just informative and meaningful, but also works of artistic beauty. These photographs allow us to see the ancient towns, fortresses and villages, within the setting of their landscapes, with roads winding off into the distance, with agricultural fields and stone terraces extending up the slopes of hills and down deep into the valleys and in every direction. Some of these pictures are breathtaking and one can simply sit back and enjoy their beauty, or, alternatively, one can use them to reflect and provide insight on the long history of the Land of Israel, extending back into the mists of time.

We hope you will enjoy this book.

Early Hellenistic	Late Hellenistic	Early Roman	Late Roman	Byzantine	Umayyad	Abbasid	Crusader/ Ayyubid	Ayyubid/ Mamluk	Ottoman to Modern
332-167	167-37	37-135	135-325	325-638	638-750	750-1099	1099-1291	1291-1561	1517-1917
B.C.E	B.C.E	B.C.E/C.E.	C.E.	C.E.	C.E.	C.E.	C.E.	C.E.	

Part One:

PREHISTORIC BEGINNINGS

"Possession of a great capacity for this conceptual thinking, in contrast to the mainly perceptual thinking of apes and other primates, is generally regarded by comparative psychologists as distinctive of man. Systematic making of tools implies a marked capacity for conceptual thought."
(Kenneth P. Oakley, Man the Tool–Maker. Chicago, 1961).

More than one million years ago small bands of creatures of proto-human appearance (Homo erectus) roamed the Levant, moving carefully along the edges of marshy inland valleys, padding their way next to lakes, across the Carmel Hills and deep into the heavily wooded hills of Galilee. They were quite hairy, of gaunt appearance, with deep-set eyes and swinging long arms. They communicated with each other by grunts and a rudimentary form of sign language. They constantly sought food, either by collecting berries and root plants, or by killing small animals, reptiles and birds. They warily approached the mangled carcasses of large mammals left by sated predators at kill sites, to see if they could scavenge bits of meat or suck out the marrow of discarded bones, but they were always on their guard and danger was always just around the corner. The flesh was eaten raw, scraped off bones with fragments of flint and stone, slightly sharpened. Meat was only roasted in fireplaces later on when the use of fire for cooking purposes first began to be appreciated. Sleeping was done on the ground, huddling together for warmth and as a protection against aggressive large animals looking for their next meal. It was a tough life and it was survival only for the fittest.

Below and far right: views of the 'Ubeidiya landscape during different seasons of the year.

Ubeidiya

At first glance 'Ubeidiya seems to be a very unpromising archaeological site, at least for visitors. Making our way along the beaten track leading from the dig house, we passed piles of rubble and soil, covered with unruly thistles and yellowing weeds and grass. It was hot and many flies were buzzing around our heads. Our guide, the prehistorian, Eitan Tchernov, was not at all perturbed. Eventually, we turned a corner and passed along a ridge and there in front of us we could see an excavation area with an exposure of scattered flint tools and animal bones dating back some 1.4 to 1.0 million years before present. It was breathtaking.

The site is situated not far from the west bank of the Jordan River, where it exits from the Sea of Galilee, and is named after an unexcavated historical mound in the vicinity. Owing to the geological folding and faulting of the land, some of the finds appear in almost vertical layers of local lacustrine and fluvial deposits, which is quite bizarre and takes getting used to. Originally the site was on the edge of a small sweet–water lake; this accounts for the abundance of bones of mammals, reptiles, fish and birds. Bones were also found of hippopotamus, horse and deer. The hominids living at the site were hunters and scavengers; they made distinctive chopping tools of flint and spheroids of limestone, as well as hand–axes of flint and to a lesser degree of basalt. Some of the hand–axes looked natural but they were undoubtedly shaped purposefully.

Two prehistoric hand–axes from the excavations.

'Ubeidiya is a key site for understanding what was happening in the Levant when the proto–human Homo erectus began moving into the region from Africa during the Lower Acheulean stage of the Lower Palaeolithic age.

A general view of Nahal Amud where ez-Zuttiyeh cave is located with the Sea of Galilee behind. *Opposite:* views of the prehistoric caves in the Carmel hills.

Prehistoric Caves in the Galilee and Carmel

Nahal Amud
Carmel

Little did the young Englishman Francis Turville–Petre know when he began digging at the cave of ez–Zuttiyeh (the "robber's cave") in 1925 in the eastern hills of Galilee, that he was on the verge of making a major archaeological discovery of lasting importance. From deep in the ground, beneath blocks of fallen stone, Turville–Petre extracted a fragmentary human skull of enormous antiquity. Even today, the "Galilee Skull", as it is now known, is regarded as the oldest human fossil ever found in the Levant. The Carmel Caves have also produced remarkable remains dating from the Middle and Upper Palaeolithic periods. The Mousterians of the Middle Palaeolithic were hunter–and–gatherers, quite adept at producing refined cutting tools for butchering meat and sawing bones, and for processing animal skins. They were also good at woodworking and hafting tools, such as fixing "Levallois" points to wooden spears. Skeletal remains found in the Tabun and Kebara Caves indicate they belonged to Neanderthals, though whether these were migrants or a local Mediterranean population is still unknown.

Shifting climatic changes towards the end of the Pleistocene era (circa 12,800 B.C.E) saw the emergence of a local sedentary culture known as Natufian. Settlement was in front of caves and along terraces. Houses were round or oval and some of them contained hearths and work areas with grinding vessels. Burials – usually flexed or stretched–out interments – have been uncovered in excavations beneath the houses or adjacent courtyards. Some of the artistic objects that have been unearthed are exceptionally beautiful, notably carved heads on sickle shafts and necklaces and bracelets made of *Dentalium* shells and pendants of semi–precious stone and bone.

14

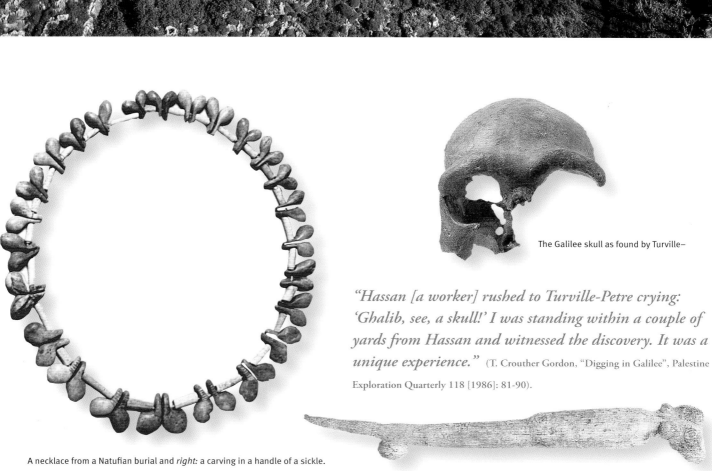

A necklace from a Natufian burial and *right:* a carving in a handle of a sickle.

The Galilee skull as found by Turville–

"Hassan [a worker] rushed to Turville-Petre crying: 'Ghalib, see, a skull!' I was standing within a couple of yards from Hassan and witnessed the discovery. It was a unique experience." (T. Crouther Gordon, "Digging in Galilee", Palestine Exploration Quarterly 118 [1986]: 81-90).

Jericho (Tell es-Sultan)

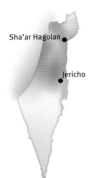

Defined by Dame Kathleen Kenyon in the 1950s as the "world's oldest city", the prominent mound of Jericho – known in Arabic as Tell es–Sultan – remains one of the most fascinating ancient sites in the Levant. Situated in an oasis in the lower Jordan Valley, just north of the Dead Sea, substantial remains have been uncovered from the Neolithic, Bronze and Iron Ages, but nothing at all to suggest that there was any city at this location (except ruins) when the Israelites passed into the Promised Land under the leadership of Joshua Ben Nun (Josh. 6:1).

An important discovery at Jericho was that of a massive round tower (8.5 metres high) with an internal staircase, attached to a wall segment fronted by a rock–cut ditch (3.5 meters wide). They were dated to the Pre–Pottery stage of the Neolithic period, to the 8th millennium B.C.E. Kenyon thought they were fortifications and that they were built to defend the settlers; other prehistorians, however, have suggested they were part of a barrier which was built in order to prevent flooding of the town and that the round tower was the lower part of a mud–brick shrine (no longer extant). The debate continues.

Kenyon was a fierce adherent of correct and exacting methods of archaeological excavation and even wrote a book on methods of digging. Hence, when a human skull became partly exposed in the earthen section of her dig at Jericho in 1953, she refused to have it dug out: "one never goes burrowing about an ancient site just to remove things… So there we left it". At the end of the dig, Kenyon relented and allowed her dig supervisor, Peter Parr, to dig out the skull, since, as she wrote, "remains of Neolithic men are too important to be ignored." The skull turned out to be one of seven skulls with plaster–molded features and with eyes inset with shells. Plastered skulls have been found at other sites of the Pre–Pottery stage of the Neolithic and it has been suggested that they represent stylized representations of ancestors, but recent research does not support claims that age, sex or skull shape were domineering factors in the choice of skulls for special treatment.

"Peter Parr, in charge of digging in that area, appeared that evening with an astonishing object. It was a Neolithic skull all right, but the whole of the lower part was covered with plaster molded into human features… One of these sculptured skulls would have been culmination enough for our two seasons' work, but more surprises were in store. Visible in the cavity from which Parr had removed the first skull lay two others. When these were removed, three more appeared. Behind them lay still another." (K. M. Kenyon and A. D. Tushingham, "Jericho Gives Up Its Secrets", The National Geographic Magazine Vol. 104, 6, [1953]: 853-870.

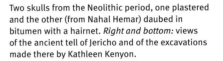

Two skulls from the Neolithic period, one plastered and the other (from Nahal Hemar) daubed in bitumen with a hairnet. *Right and bottom:* views of the ancient tell of Jericho and of the excavations made there by Kathleen Kenyon.

In 1983 archaeologist David Alon stumbled across a cave on the right-hand bank of Nahal Hemar in the Judean Desert. The cave was asymmetrical in appearance, with fissures in the roof and large fallen boulders scattered on its floor. An amazing array of artifacts and organic remains from the Neolithic period were uncovered beneath the rubble, notably skulls coated with asphalt, fragments of stone masks, flint knives, and ropes and baskets.

Sha'ar Hagolan

The Neolithic peoples of the Levant quickly established themselves in permanent villages. They survived by herding animals and cultivating crops. Agricultural surpluses, if there were any, were used to trade for exotic items. Some of these commodities came from great distances (up to 700 kilometres away): obsidian (volcanic glass) from eastern Turkey and marine shells from the Red Sea. One of the flourishing villages of this period (the Pottery stage of the Neolithic: sixth–fifth millennia B.C.E.) was situated on the northern bank of the Yarmuk River in the central Jordan Valley, close to the modern kibbutz (an Israeli collective village) of Sha'ar Hagolan from which it got its name. Three blocks of dwellings with courtyards separated by alleys were uncovered by an archaeological team, indicating that the village was not built haphazardly but with a certain degree of advance planning; at 20 hectares this village is one of the largest of its period in the world.

Sha'ar Hagolan turned out to be very rich in art objects: more than three hundred objects were found, some schematic carvings on pebbles, but many more of female figurines made out of fired clay, probably representing the great Mother Goddess. Some of these objects are now exhibited in the Metropolitan Museum of New York and in the Louvre Museum in Paris.

A pebble figurine with incised eyes and *right:* a seated female figurine from Sha'ar Hagolan.

Biq'at Uvda

On the floor of the desert at Biq'at Uvda, to the west of the Arabah, is a scene of six leopards attacking a lone oryx or antelope. Nearby are representations of six more animals, of which two are identified as leopards with cubs. These remarkable images (known as geoglyphs) were made on the desert floor using small stones set upright and the only way of looking at them is from the air. Since they were evidently not made to be seen by the earthbound, they were probably created to attract the gods, or to placate them. The drawings are assumed to date to the same time as the nearby temple which was excavated and dated to the late sixth millennium B.C.E.

The Sinai leopard (*Panthera pardus jarvisi*) was mentioned in a number of biblical passages (e.g. Habbakuk 1:8; Hosea 13:7), but was thought to have become extinct in Israel until a chance observation of the animal was made in 1974 in the cliffs above En Gedi near the Dead Sea. The leopard was regarded as a sacred animal in some parts of the Near East, and wall paintings depicting the cult of the leopard were unearthed at the Neolithic site of Çatal Hüyük in Turkey.

The temple at Biq'at Uvda with the animal drawings made of stones on the ground in the foreground.

"Can the Ethiopian change his skin, or the leopard change its spots? Then may ye also do good, that are accustomed to do evil." (Jeremiah 13:23)

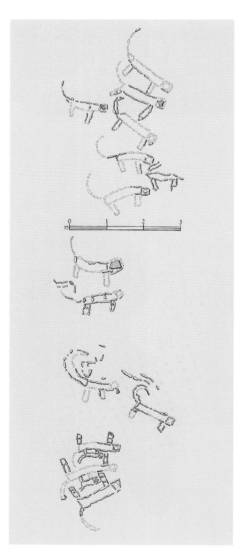

An artist's rendering of these stone drawings.

An additional site with enclosed rooms in Biq'at Uvda.

En Gedi

High up on the mountain, not far from the spring of En Gedi, archaeologists in the 1950s came across the remains of stone structures protected by an enclosure wall in which there was a small gateway. The site would have made a perfect location for a shrine, perched as it was on a natural hill terrace with a magnificent view of the En Gedi oasis and the sultry expanse of the Dead Sea to the east. Not surprisingly, subsequent excavations in this place brought to light the remains of a temple dating from the fourth millennium B.C.E. and within the structure pottery, animal bones and ashes were uncovered, as well as a clay figurine of a bull carrying a churn on its back.

The cultic objects from this temple may very well have been hidden in the nearby Nahal Mishmar cave. This cave produced an amazing cache of 442 different objects made of copper, haematite, stone and ivory (of hippopotamus and elephant). In the courtyard of the En Gedi temple a circular installation was found and recently it has been suggested that it might have served to protect the lower trunk of a tree. Sacred trees were a familiar component of religious practice in the ancient Near East throughout the ages and are mentioned in the Old Testament as well.

"Ye shall utterly destroy all the places, wherein the nations which ye shall possess served their gods, upon the high mountains, and upon the hills, and under every green tree" (Deuteronomy 12:2).

A ceramic bull figurine from the shrine and a copper basket–shaped vessel found in the Nahal Mishmar

Bottom right and top: the Chalcolithic shrine on the cliff overlooking the oasis of En Gedi, with a closer view of the circular stone installation in its courtyard.

Below and lower right: the mysterious monument of concentric circles at Rujm el-Hiri.

One of many dolmen found in fields in the Golan Heights.

Rujm el-Hiri

Everyone likes a mystery and the magnificent megalithic site of Rujm el–Hiri (which in Arabic means "stone heap of the wild cat"), situated on the central plateau of the Golan Heights, seems like it must go back to the age of the gods. It consists of a set of stone–built concentric circles, the outermost 156 meters in diameter, with the rings sporadically connected by short radial walls. In the early twentieth century, monocentric hyper–diffusionists, such as G. Elliot Smith, thought such megalithic structures were created by a super–race of migrating "Children of the Sun" from Egypt in the process of making their way towards Europe. Nowadays we know these diffusionists got it wrong, but the modern fascination with megalithics and stone circles and the reasons for their construction remains and their scientific study has not abated. The current thinking is that the circles of Rujm el–Hiri were part of an Early Bronze Age ceremonial center for observing celestial and non–celestial phenomena. Its monumentality served to reflect the controlling power of the society that was in charge of the "enclosure" settlements of the third–millennium B.C.E. in the Golan.

Surrounding the circle of Rujm el–Hiri are many hundreds of dolmens ("stone table" in Breton, from *dol*, "table", and *men*, "stone") which are ancient burial chambers constructed of undressed vertical stone slabs, usually weighing several tons, supporting a single flat capstone. Burial in dolmens, or within stone cairns or tumuli, is characteristic of the southern Levant during much of the late fourth and third millennia B.C.E. They are characteristic of regions where the geology does not provide natural caves or where the rock is difficult to quarry. Dolmens usually appear in groups ('fields') and they number in the hundreds. Variation in monument type has been noted within the dolmen fields suggesting the existence of a hierarchy within the populations they served. The general consensus of opinion is that dolmens served populations from a non–sedentary pastoralist background.

"Little need we wonder, then, when the certainty of revolving seasons even was not yet a matter beyond dispute, and when time was measured by days and nights, the shepherds and primitive agriculturalists looked anxiously for the time when the wintry sun should begin to retrace his course, or marked with apprehension his return southwards on the horizon – little need we marvel that they erected monuments which could serve as rude means of measuring the movement of the sacred orb…" (C.R. Conder, Heth and Moab, 1883, pp. 217-218).

A general view of site showing the city enclosed within a fortification wall with projecting semi-circular towers. The water-well is situated in the center-right of the picture and the Iron Age citadel may be seen in the background.

The Development of Early Cities

The Early Bronze Age (3rd millennium B.C.E.) saw the emergence of fully–fledged cities in the Land of Israel for the first time, with massive fortifications and city–gates, distinct built–up neighborhoods set aside for housing, industrial and mercantile activities, administrative complexes/palaces, temples, silos and public water systems. The reasons for the development of urbanism at this point of time are unclear. What is certain, however, is that cities became larger and denser than the earlier villages and they appear to have wielded greater political control over their hinterland, enabling them to tap the surpluses derived from agricultural produce – particularly olive oil and wheat – for their own benefit. The smaller number of settlements of this period does not mean a decrease in population but implies that more people were moving from the countryside into the developing cities of Canaan. This ultimately led to a differentiation between the status and function of individual villages, depending in many cases on their proximity to the roads leading to the markets, and also to the manner of their subjugation as tax–paying satellites of the various city states. All administration and agricultural activities were now administered directly from the cities by the rulers and their officials.

A potsherd found at the site with a *serekh* of Narmer incised on it.

Arad

Arad is an excellent example of a large fortified Early Bronze Age city situated in the eastern Negev Desert. It was a well–planned city divided into neighborhoods by streets, with shrines (one with a stele depicting deities or worshippers with upraised arms), public or palace buildings, a water system (with a depth of at least 15 meters), and surrounded by a massive fortification wall with projecting semi–circular towers. The houses were of a distinctive broad–room plan (hence the "Arad house") with the entrance in the long wall. The pottery vessels from the site include some imported from Egypt, as well as a large quantity of local painted and burnished wares some of which have been found in First Dynasty tombs at Abydos. A potsherd was also dug up incised with the Egyptian King Narmer's Horus (sacred falcon) name. Narmer was either the last king of the Proto–dynastic period or the first king of the First Dynasty of Egypt; the matter is still debated by scholars. In any case, this potsherd provides an important synchronism between Egypt and Canaan.

"I hypothesize that urbanization is the result of the stimulus provided by a centralized political system, often referred to as a 'state' organization, rather than of a particular level of technological development as such. Of course, a relatively high level of productivity is necessary before centralized political control can be achieved, but an advanced technology by itself – without the stimulation of a state organization – will not give rise to urbanization."

(Robert F. Heizer, American Antiquity 26 [1960]: 215-222).

An ancient ceramic model of a typical "Arad house".

Top and bottom: the sprawling site of the Early Bronze city of Yarmuth, with *(top)* one of the excavated buildings in the foreground. *Below:* A female figurine perhaps cultic in origin.

Yarmuth

Quite possibly this site may have been the Canaanite "city of Yaramu" mentioned in a fourteenth–century clay tablet. One of its kings, Piram, fought and died in battle during the war of the Amorites against Gibeon (Joshua 10: 3-5; 23, 12: 11). But long before all this happened, the city flourished during the Early Bronze Age (third millennium B.C.E.) and judging by its size (36 acres) it must have been a very important city in the central foothills region of the Shephelah. Excavations have been conducted in the area of the Lower City revealing amazing monumental architecture without parallel in the archaeology of the period, notably massive fortifications with an offset gateway, sanctuaries (of which one is known as the "white building"), palaces, and numerous large and spacious dwellings indicating that the inhabitants enjoyed a pleasant lifestyle.

Ashkelon

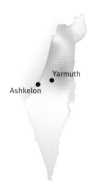

Ashkelon has been described as one of the oldest and most important archaeological sites in the Holy Land on the shore of the Mediterranean Sea. And this is definitely true. The ancient mound, which is now part of a national park to which Israelis flock to picnic on its grassy knolls and to laze around on its adjacent sandy beach, has archaeological remains from almost every single period in the history of the country from prehistoric times and as late as the Ottoman period. Ashkelon has had a fascinating history. Mentioned in the Execration Texts of the 19th century B.C.E. as *Ascanu*, it was for a while a Canaanite city–state under Egyptian influence, and its capture by Rameses II was portrayed vividly on a relief in the Temple of Karnak in Egypt. In the Old Testament it was referred to as one of the five principal cities of the Philistines (Joshua 13:3). The first person to excavate at Ashkelon was the eccentric Lady Hester Stanhope in 1814, who was seeking hidden treasure but found instead a Roman statue which she then proceeded to break into pieces and throw into the sea. Subsequent scientific excavations revealed little of the prehistoric levels, but major ramparts dating from the Middle Bronze Age have been traced including a city gate with the oldest monumental arches hitherto discovered in the Near East (c. 2000 B.C.E.). The gate was built of mud–brick and had a narrow passageway flanked by towers. Contemporary with the latest phase of the rampart and gate is a shrine, named by the excavators the "Sanctuary of the Silver Calf", and based on a silver–coated bronze statuette found in it.

A group of cultic statuettes bearing the hallmarks of Egyptian influence.

The Egyptian Stele of Merenptah (13th century B.C.E.): "Destruction for Tehenu! Hatti is pacified; Canaan is plundered with every evil; Ashkelon is taken; Gezer is captured; Yanoam is made non-existent; Israel lies desolate; its seed is no more; Hurru has become a widow for To-meri; All the lands in their entirety are at peace, Everyone who was a nomad has been curbed by King Merenptah." (D. Winton Thomas, Documents From Old Testament Times. New York, 1961, p.139)

Top and bottom: the Middle Bronze Age gate of the city, seen at the time of the excavations and *(below)* after a sloping roof had been built to protect it.

"And the men of the city [Ashkelon] said unto him [Samson] on the seventh day before the sun went down: What is sweeter than honey? And what is stronger than a lion? And he said unto them: If ye had not plowed with my heifer, ye had not found out my riddle. And the Spirit of the Lord came upon him and he went down to Ashkelon and slew thirty of them, and took their spoil, and gave change of garments unto them which expounded the riddle." (Judges 14: 18-19).

The important agricultural calendar
dating from the 10th century B.C.E.

Gezer

Gezer is mentioned as a prominent site in the
Egyptian accounts of Thutmosis III and IV in
the fifteenth century B.C.E. It is not surprising,
therefore, that the excavations made at the site by
R.A.S. Macalister uncovered remains of a Middle
Bronze Age city from that period, including an
area with a mysterious row of ten monolithic
standing stones (similar to the biblical *masseboth*)
which archaeologists think may have been part of
a sacred "high place".

Gezer is situated at a strategic location, guarding
the junction between the Via Maris (the "Way of the Sea") and
the trunk road extending past Gezer to the Valley of Aijalon
where Joshua made the moon stand still (Joshua 10: 12-13). The
fact that this mound is indeed Gezer and not some other site,
is confirmed by the Arabic name of the site – Tell el–Jazari – as
well as by the discovery in the nearby fields of Roman boundary
inscriptions cut into the rock, reading *tehum gezer* ("boundary of
Gezer") in Hebrew and in Greek the name of the estate owner,
Alkiou.

Gezer is also well–known for its well preserved fortification walls
and gates, one of which is dated to the time of King Solomon
(10th century B.C.E.), although some scholars have been pressing
for a slightly later date. An important discovery made during
Macalister's excavations in 1908 was that of the so–called "Gezer
Calendar" on a limestone plaque which is dated to the late 10th
century B.C.E. and provides details about the agricultural year; it
indicates that in biblical times the farmer's lot was undoubtedly a
tough one.

*The following is the text of the 10th
century B.C.E. Gezer Calendar: "Two
months of ingathering, two months of
sowing, two months of late sowing, one
month of chopping flax, one month of
barley harvest, one month of harvest
and completion, two months of grape
cutting, one month of summer fruits."*

The High Place at Gezer with its prominent standing stones and the blur of a cyclist along the adjacent path.

Stone inscribed with an inscription reading "boundary of Gezer". *Left:* a gold artifact from the excavations at the site.

"The results of the week's trial [in the area of the standing stones] being thus so stimulating, it was resolved to transfer the whole body of labourers from the Eastern Hill, where they were at the time working, to the neighbourhood of the standing stones; and large pits were laid out for excavation north and south of the stones, so as to expose a sufficient area around them… Before very long the characteristic remains of the now famous High Place were unearthed one by one. By a fortnight all the stones of the alignment had been exposed, and the two northernmost surviving, which had fallen, were re-erected." (R.A.S. Macalister, The Excavation of Gezer, Vol. I, 1912, p. 51)

Aphek

Dominated by an Ottoman fort, the mound of Tel Aphek was the focus of an archaeological project conducted by the Tel Aviv University. Digging operations there led to the discovery of significant remains of palaces dating from the Middle Bronze and Late Bronze Ages (2nd millennium B.C.E.). Archaeologists found the excavation of the Late Bronze Age palace particularly exciting: it comprised a spacious building containing many rooms, with a staircase tower which gave access to rooms on an upper story where the rulers of Aphek lived. Courts and service buildings surrounded the main palace building; many grape pips and the presence of wine presses surely indicates that the rulers of Aphek (and perhaps also their servants) enjoyed drinking wine and in quantity.

An amazing and unexpected discovery in the ruins of the palace, which was destroyed at the end of the 13th century B.C.E., were numerous Egyptian, Hittite and Akkadian clay documents, among them a Sumerian–Akkadian dictionary, and a fragment of a unique trilingual Sumerian–Akkadian–Canaanite dictionary. This is the only multilingual document hitherto found which includes the Canaanite language.

A general view of the Ottoman fort at Aphek *(top)* and one area of the excavations.

"In the collapse of the upper story of the Governor's palace, together with everyday objects that were buried beneath the ruins, a considerable number of written documents were found, a discovery that may be considered rare and valuable in the archaeology of the Land of Israel of biblical times. The documents were scattered in different parts of the palace, and sometimes were even found to have fallen beneath the rubble extending outside its boundary walls."

(M. Kochavi, Aphek–Antipatris: Five Thousand Years of History, 1989, p. 69).

Jerishe

The approximate shape of many of the ancient mounds of the Land of Israel was already fully determined in the Middle Bronze Age, and this because the cities were surrounded for the first time by massive earthen or stone glacis ramparts which were engineering features that made these sites stand out within their natural landscapes. Tel Jerishe, situated close to the junction of the Yarkon and Ayalon Rivers, in north Tel Aviv, is one such mound whose general shape was determined in the Middle Bronze Age. In addition to the fortifications, archaeological excavations also brought to light an impressive water system consisting of a circular shaft with steps leading down to the water source. Today the site is hemmed in on all sides by modern buildings but because the site is registered as a place of antiquity, no modern construction will be allowed either on the mound or on its slopes.

A view of Tel Jerishe hemmed in by modern buildings.

At the moment 91 cuneiform tablets and objects have been found in the Land of Israel, some of them deriving from the Bronze Age cities of Canaan (such as Aphek), and others from the cities of the Philistines, as well as inscriptions from the Kingdoms of Judah and Israel.

Two cuneiform tablets and *(left)* a stamped Hittite seal from Aphek.

Bottom and top right: views of the mound of Beth Shean with the excavated remains of an ancient bridge in the foreground (*bottom*).

Beth Shean

In the courtyard of a Late Bronze Age temple at Beth Shean a remarkable discovery was made: a large fallen statue of an Egyptian pharaoh in two pieces. It turned out to be a provincial–style carving of Rameses III made out of black basalt. It was not the kind of find that regularly turns up at archaeological sites in Israel.

But there were more remarkable discoveries made nearby: the stele of Rameses II and another one of Seti I. Archaeologists think these artifacts came from earlier levels at the site, that they were vandalized and then chucked into this courtyard, perhaps with the destruction of Beth Shean in the late 12th century B.C.E. The "large" stele of Seti I, for example, dates to the 13th century B.C.E. and relates how three Egyptian military units were successful in quelling a local rebellion which took place in the northern Jordan Valley; it mentions various place–names including Pella, Rehov, Yenoam and, of course, also Beth Shean. The "small" stele of Seti I describes a military campaign that was made against the *habiru* (vagabonds) situated in the hill country.

All of these artifacts indicate the primary importance of Beth Shean as an Egyptian administrative center in the northern part of the country during the Nineteenth Egyptian Dynasty. According to the Old Testament Beth Shean was later inhabited by the Philistines at least until the time of King David; it was the place where the beheaded body of the vanquished King Saul was displayed on the city wall. Archaeology, however, has failed to reveal evidence for a Philistine occupation at the site.

Statue of Rameses III and a stele of Seti I 14th century B.C.E.

"And when the inhabitants of Jabesh Gilead heard of that which the Philistines had done to Saul; All the valiant men arose, and went all night, and took the body of Saul and the bodies of his sons from the wall of Beth Shean, and came to Jabesh and burnt them there." (I Samuel 31: 12-13)

31

Hazor

Amnon Ben–Tor, the director of the dig at Hazor, has not found the hidden archives of clay documents from the Middle or Late Bronze Ages yet, even though the search has been on for quite a few years. "One or two cuneiform tablet fragments have actually come to light", Ben–Tor says, "suggesting we're definitely within the 'bank', even though we haven't been able to lay our hands on the 'safe' yet."

In the center of Area A at the top of the upper city (the acropolis) recent excavations brought to light an impressive and well preserved Late Bronze Age administrative building or palace – of *bit hilani* type – with walls built of solid mud–brick laced with cedar–beams above a foundation course of massive smoothed blocks of basalt (orthostats). The evidence is that this building was destroyed between 1270 and 1250 B.C.E., though who was responsible for this destruction is unknown. What is certain is that the subsequent Israelites who settled at the site built flimsy stone dwellings on top of the ruined city and inexplicably dug circular "rubbish" pits in almost every nook and cranny.

Tell Hazor is one of the largest artificial mounds in the Land of Israel. In the Old Testament it features in the account of the conquests of Joshua (Joshua 11: 10-13). It is also recorded that it became one of the royal cities built by Solomon, together with the sites of Megiddo and Gezer (1 Kings 9: 15). Excavations were conducted at Hazor by the famous Israeli general, politician and archaeologist Yigael Yadin in the 1950s and have been renewed since 1990 by Amnon Ben–Tor. Yadin's excavations in one area of the site brought to light an amazing sequence of superimposed shrines from the 14th and 13th centuries B.C.E. They contain numerous upright standing stones (*stelae*), one depicting hands stretched upwards towards a crescent, and statues of a lion and of a man.

"*It was clearly a miniature sanctuary: the statue was small, the stelae were small. But we were so bewildered and excited about the discovery that everything looked big... When we deepened the dig just in front of and below the statue, we found the head of the statue, which exactly fitted the torso...*"

(Y. Yadin, Hazor: The Rediscovery of a Great Citadel of the Bible, 1975, p. 43).

Late Bronze Age stelae with a statue of seated man, and the acropolis of Hazor *(right)* with the lower city behind.

The copper–mining district of Timna with a circular rock–cut installation in the foreground.

"Then there passed by Midianites merchantmen; and they drew and lifted up Joseph out of the pit, and sold Joseph to the Ishmaelites for twenty pieces of silver: and they brought Joseph into Egypt." (Genesis 37: 28). A

Top Right: the Egyptian goddess Hathor carved in white sandstone.
Bottom: a copper animal figurine.

Timna

At the foot of majestic reddish cliffs within the baking hot Timna Valley to the north of the modern town of Eilat, archaeologists uncovered in 1969 the remains of an Egyptian shrine at the very center of an ancient copper mining district, inaccurately referred to by some as "King Solomon's Mines". In the Late Bronze Age (14th–12th centuries B.C.E.) the Egyptians exploited this region for its copper and their activities brought them into contact with the Canaanites of Palestine and the mysterious Midianites from the Arabian Peninsula. The temple was small, with a stone bench for offerings and with *stelae* set against one of its walls. During its final stage the temple was probably covered by a large tent instead of having a permanent roof. Cut into the side of a square pillar were images of the Egyptian goddess Hathor. Thousands of unique objects and carvings were found during the excavations, many of them of great beauty. The first group includes Egyptian–made objects, some of which bear hieroglyphic inscriptions and royal cartouches from the 19th and 20th Dynasties. The second group consists of locally–made objects, as well as a type of painted pottery whose origin was probably Midianite. Copper objects include a cast figurine of a male god with phallus, and an alluring snake with a gilded head.

The excavator, Beno Rothenberg, planned to excavate at the site for only two weeks, but because of the spectacular nature of the finds eventually worked at the temple for two months, uncovering almost 10,000 objects including hundreds of tiny beads, very fragile faience, glass and wooden objects, and even decayed cloth.

The Hathor temple at the foot of the cliffs.

Three Midianite decorated ceramic vessels.

35

Part Two:

EMERGENCE OF THE ISRAELITES

*"And this is the reason for the levy which King Solomon
raised; for to build the House of the Lord, and his
own house, and Millo, and the wall of Jerusalem, and
Hazor, Megiddo, and Gezer." (I Kings 9: 15)*

Where the Israelites came from and by what means they managed to establish themselves within the country, later known as the Land of Israel, is a matter that has been seriously debated by scholars, and no one is in agreement. The traditional view (Numbers 33: 3-15) is that Moses led the People of Israel out of slavery in Egypt, in an exodus that took them to Mount Sinai and on a trek through the Sinai desert for forty years, and then, finally, under the guidance of Joshua Ben Nun, they entered the "Land of Milk and Honey", conquering local cities in their wake.

The archaeological evidence reveals a somewhat different scenario, signaling a certain amount of cultural continuity in the Early Iron Age with that of previous Late Bronze Age cultural traditions, even though there was definitely a major shift in settlement patterns, particularly in the highland regions of the country. Early Iron Age settlements (from circa 1200 B.C.E.) were modest in appearance, unfortified with small stone-built structures, animal pens and some agricultural terracing.

What is certain is that by the tenth or ninth centuries B.C.E., at the time of the United Monarchy, one witnesses the emergence of cities with all the signs of fully-fledged statehood: large gates and massive fortification walls, impressive monumental pillared buildings, public silos, and deep water systems. The reference in I Kings 9 to the construction of the royal cities of Solomon – Hazor, Megiddo and Gezer – is seen by some scholars to reflect this process of statehood formation.

A pensive deity
from Qitmit.

Top and bottom: the acropolis of 'Ai with the softly-curved hills behind, and the foundations of an Early Bronze Age temple.

'Ai (et-Tell)

"Ai was excavated by a woman", was the startling way that archaeologist Shmuel Yeivin chose to begin his lecture about the excavations at the site while visiting London in the 1960s. The audience tittered. Yeivin, of course, knew all about the site since he had worked there with the French archaeologist J. Marquet-Krause in 1933-35. Marquet-Krause was an excellent archaeologist and her archaeological conclusions about the site remained firm, even after the site was re-excavated by J. Callaway in 1964.

During her campaigns at the site (et-Tell, identified as biblical 'Ai: Joshua 8:1-29), Marquet-Krause managed to uncover important remains of a very large Early Bronze Age city from the third millennium B.C.E., with a number of large buildings, including a temple, and fortifications.

No Late Bronze Age settlement was discovered at the site, thus casting doubt on the accuracy of the biblical text mentioning that Joshua burnt 'Ai.

In the Early Iron Age, however, the lower city was left in an abandoned state – the name 'Ai in Hebrew means 'ruin' – and only a very small village was established on a terraced level under the acropolis to the northeast.

Shiloh

The hill of Shiloh is extremely stony. In later times, the many thousands of stones scattered across the site were gathered into piles or shifted to form boundary walls, or to construct barrier walls next to paths, and then farmers began plowing and cultivating the land, with varying degrees of success.

These agricultural attempts to eke out a means of subsistence from the ground meant that farmers would have been confronted with evidences from the past on a daily basis: segments of walls from ancient dwellings poking out of the ground, broken potsherds, caves and installations, and tombs. This, after all, was the site of Shiloh (in Arabic Khirbet Seilun), the place where, according to tradition, the Ark of the Covenant was kept (Joshua 18:1; I Samuel 1:3) before it was lost in battle to the Philistines at Aphek (I Samuel 4).

A general view of Shiloh showing the excavated areas between the agricultural plots.

Archaeological excavations at the site indicate that Shiloh in the Early Iron Age consisted of numerous dwellings, courtyards, pillared buildings, and silos for the storage of agricultural produce. Many collared rim jars, typical of the period, were also found. The shrine was probably originally situated at the top of the hill, but, unfortunately this area is exposed and its appearance is now unclear. It might have been a permanent building (I Samuel 3:15) or it might have been a platform for a portable shrine (II Samuel 7:6). We shall probably never know.

Joshua burnt Ai, and made it a heap for ever, even a desolation unto this day. And the king of Ai he hanged on a tree until eventide: and as soon as the sun was down, Joshua commanded that they should take his carcase down from the tree, and cast it at the entering of the gate of the city, and raise thereon a great heap of stones, that remaineth unto this day"

(Joshua 8: 28-29)

A typical agricultural terrace on the slope of a hill.

Terrace cultivation: Terraces built in serried fashion on the slopes of hills are ubiquitous in the highland regions of the Land of Israel. They were constructed in order to increase areas that might be used by farmers for agriculture since the areas in the wadi beds are narrow and limited in area. The earliest terraces have been dated back to the beginning of the Early Bronze Age, but large scale terrace construction apparently only took place from the 8th century B.C.E. onwards. Most of the terraces one can see today were built in the Roman and Byzantine periods, with reconstruction work taking place until modern times.

Various artifacts from Philistine sites: a seated figurine ("Ashdoda" type), a cultic stand from Ashdod (*top left*) and an Assyrian bottle from Batash (*top right*).

Ashdod
Batash

The World of the Philistines

They were not at all boorish, as their name might seem to imply. On the contrary, based on archaeological remains, we know they were an extremely cultured and refined group of people. The Philistines were regarded as the arch-enemies of the Israelites in the biblical text and are the *Peleshet* mentioned in Egyptian texts on the walls of the Medinet Habu temple in Thebes from the time of Rameses III (c. 1185 B.C.E.). Part of an extremely interesting population movement (known as the "Sea Peoples") which took place at the beginning of the first millennium B.C.E., the Philistines eventually established themselves in the southern limits of the Levant (Joshua 13:3; I Samuel 6:17), close to the Mediterranean Sea, with an urban culture focused on five major cities (a pentapolis), namely Gaza, Ashdod, Ashkelon, Ekron (Tel Miqne) and Gath (Tell es-Safi), with important remains also found at Tel Qasile and Tel Batash (Timna?). The distinctive material culture of the Philistines which was derived from Aegean origins, rapidly absorbed foreign (i.e. Egyptian and Cypriot) and local Canaanite influences. Important remains of the Philistine kingdom, which existed parallel to the Israelite kingdoms during the Iron Age (c. 1200 – 586 B.C.E), have been found at Ekron (Tel Miqne) and Gath (Tell es-Safi), as well as at Ashkelon and Ashdod.

Top and bottom: the mounds of Batash and Ashdod.

"Now there was no smith found throughout all the Land of Israel: for the Philistines said, Lest the Hebrews make them swords or spears. But all the Israelites went down to the Philistines, to sharpen every man his share, and his coulter, and his axe, and his mattock. Yet they had a file for the mattocks, and for the coulters, and for the forks, and for the axes, and to sharpen the goads." (I Samuel 13: 19-21).

Ekron (Miqne)

Absolute confirmation that Tel Miqne (Khirbat el-Muqanna') was indeed the Philistine city of Ekron came to light in the summer of 1996 when archaeologists digging at the site uncovered a unique block of stone inscribed with four lines of Semitic writing. Visiting the site the day after the discovery, one could sense the overall excitement in the air, with diggers hovering around the spot where the discovery had been made, even though the inscription itself had already been ferried away to Jerusalem for safe-keeping and study. When scholars eventually took the stone out of the packing case, it turned out to be an important royal dedicatory inscription dating from the second quarter of the seventh century B.C.E. It refers to two kings of Ekron who are also attested in Neo-Assyrian annals, namely Padi and his son Ikausu, the builder of the temple, and importantly it identifies the site quite conclusively as Ekron. The biblical site is a large fortified mound situated to the southwest of Jerusalem on the frontier zone that once separated Philistia from Judah. Excavations were undertaken there between 1981-1996 by T. Dothan and S. Gitin, and they were able to clarify the intriguing history of the site: the Philistine city was founded in the second quarter of the twelfth century B.C.E., then destroyed by Egyptians or Israelites in the 10th century B.C.E., before recovering as a vassal city of the Assyrians after 701 B.C.E. In the seventh century Ekron achieved its zenith of economic growth, becoming one of the largest industrial centers for the mass production of olive oil yet known from antiquity.

One of many oil presses with crushing basins, and beam and weight devices, found at Ekron. *Center:* the royal dedicatory inscription mentioning two kings of Ekron.

An Egyptian style female figurine with one hand holding her breast to indicate fertility.

The exact spot where the inscription was found.

Hesi

Tell el-Hesi is the first artificial mound to have been properly excavated by archaeologists. The work was begun there by the father of Near Eastern archaeology William Matthew Flinders-Petrie in 1890 and continued by his assistant Frederick Jones Bliss in 1893. Unlike Petrie, who cut small sections in different parts of the site, Bliss decided to excavate a large chunk of the site on the north-east side of the main tell, and this deep cut is today an extremely prominent feature at the site, from the ground and especially from the air. The mound is situated to the north-east of Gaza and was occupied more or less continually from Neolithic to Ottoman times. In the Iron Age it served as a military and administrative center on the border of the Kingdom of Judah.

Left: a general view of the mound "of many cities" showing the angled cut made by Bliss in its slope. *Bottom:* recent American excavations on the other slope of the mound.

Frederick J. Bliss provides a vivid (and somewhat racist) description of one of his workers, named Salami, dancing at Tell el-Hesi after an evening meal during Ramadan: "Sword in hand, cloak flowing from his shoulders, this hideous creature would creep up like some beast of the forest; when in front of the line he would flourish his sword, crouch before the dancers, suddenly advance upon them with a thrust of the sword, retreat, fall on his knees, sway back and forth, advance again still kneeling, sway back once more, all the time emitting terrible guttural cries."

(F. J. Bliss, A Mound of Many Cities, or Tell el Hesy Excavated, 1894, p. 181).

Qasile

This important Philistine site is situated on the northern outskirts of the modern city of Tel Aviv, on the banks of the (now polluted) Yarkon River. Founded by the Philistines, the town probably dealt with maritime trade, with boats reaching Qasile along the river. Excavations brought to light large numbers of hippopotamus bones, indicating that the edges of the river were extremely swampy in parts. The town was well-planned with houses built along streets; in one area of the site an important sequence of shrines was uncovered containing a large number of unique and beautiful cult objects.

A ceramic rhyton (*top*) with its lower part decorated with an animal's head, a swan-shaped bowl (*center*), and (*bottom*) a cultic-stand modeled in the shape of a man.

The site of Qasile within the grounds of the Eretz Israel Museum near Tel Aviv.

In the 1940s a potsherd was found at Tel Qasile inscribed with Palaeo-Hebrew writing, reading: "Gold of Ophir belonging to Beth Horon thirty shekels." This inscription might well be a reference to the Ophir from where Solomon acquired 420 talents of gold (1 Kings 9: 28). Scholars are divided in regard to the location of the biblical Ophir, with some placing it in eastern Africa and particularly in Sudan, and others suggesting it might have been in far away southern Arabia.

The location of "Gath of the Philistines" at Tell es-Safi.

Safi

First excavated by British explorers in the late nineteenth century, Tell es-Safi (Tel Zafit) is an amazing archaeological site. Many believe it to be the site of the biblical "Gath of the Philistines", which, according to Israelite tradition, was a stronghold of the Anakim ("giants") with Goliath renowned among its Rephaim warriors (I Samuel 17:4, 23). At the site are the remains of one of the oldest siege-works in the world and archaeologists believe these may actually be the ones tested by King Hazael of Aram-Damascus when he laid siege to the town in c. 800 B.C.E. (II Kings 12:18), eventually destroying it. Recent excavations at the site in 2005 brought to light an extraordinary inscription: a potsherd from the 10th or early 9th centuries B.C.E. inscribed with the non-Semitic names *Alwt* and *Wlt* in Proto-Canaanite letters. The two names are etymologically related to a number of Indo-European names which some scholars believe to be the source of the name "Goliath" which is a name of non-Semitic origin. Hence, the excavators have concluded that about 100 years after the time of King David, according to the standard biblical chronology, names similar to and possibly identical to that of Goliath were in common use among the inhabitants of the town of Gath.

View of circular installation uncovered in the excavations.

Above: a potsherd inscribed with a name thought to be "Goliath". *Right:* A cultic stand.

"And as he [David] talked with them [Israelites], behold, there came up the champion, the Philistine of Gath, Goliath by name, out of the armies of the Philistines, and spake according to the same words: and David heard them. And all the men of Israel, when they saw the man, fled from him, and were sore afraid." (I Samuel 17: 23-24).

The ancient mound of Dan with the Iron Age fortifications and gateway in the foreground.

"...the masseba may perform four functions: memorial, to mark the memory of a dead person; legal, to mark a legal relationship between two or more individuals; commemorative, to commemorate an event, and more specifically, to call in mind the participants in all the honor and glory of that event; and cultic, to mark the sacred area where the deity might be found, or more narrowly, to mark that exact point where the deity is cultically immanent, where worship and sacrifice will reach the deity. It is important to note that a single stone was not limited to a single function but often carried out several at one and the same time."

(Carl F. Graesser, "Standing Stones in Ancient Palestine", Biblical Archaeologist 35, 1972, p. 37)

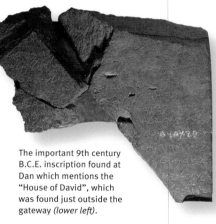

The important 9th century B.C.E. inscription found at Dan which mentions the "House of David", which was found just outside the gateway (lower left).

A remarkable ceramic Mycenean vase dating from the 14th century B.C.E. found at the site.

Cities of the North: Dan and Bethsaida

Numerous cities existed during the Iron Age in the north of the country, notably Hazor, Dan and Bethsaida, and many more. They had strong fortifications, gates, public buildings and industrial quarters. The excavations at Bethsaida brought to light a substantial gate and next to it a remarkable carved stele depicting a horned figure with a dagger in its belt. Tel Dan, in particular, situated at the source of the Jordan River, has provided numerous archaeological finds of extraordinary importance, including a dedicatory bilingual inscription in Greek and Aramaic reading "To the God who is in Dan", confirming that the identification of Tell el-Qadi as biblical Dan (1 Kings 12: 20) is indeed correct. More recently, fragments of a broken stele were discovered in the area of the city gate, dating to the 9th century B.C.E., inscribed in Aramaic and referring to the "House of David". The gate consisted of a complex of features including a stone-paved piazza with standing stones

(*masseboth*) set against the side walls. The function of these standing stones is debated, but they clearly served some purpose for those reaching the gate, perhaps cultic or commemorative. Among the numerous artifacts from the site is a beautiful Mycenaean vase from the 14th century B.C.E. depicting a chariot and horse, which was found in one of the excavated tombs.

Left: the mound of Bethsaida with the Sea of Galilee in the distance.
Bottom: a stele with a carved image of a horned god which was found next the gate at Bethsaida.

47

Tell Keisan surrounded by trees.

Keisan

Seemingly hemmed in on all sides by an army of trees, Tell Keisan is one of the largest ancient mounds in the heart of the Plain of Akko, serving as a link in the chain between the port-city of Akko (Acre), on the one hand, and inland settlements trading in wheat and other agricultural commodities, on the other. In antiquity the surrounding fertile lands were marshy, abounding in wild fowl and large game. In the Iron Age the city eventually became impoverished, and this may have been the direct result of the actions of King Hiram who declared that the towns ceded to him by Solomon (and Keisan was in that region) "did not please him" (1 Kings 9: 11-13).

Yoqne'am

At the corner of a busy intersection of two highways in the Jezreel Valley, the mound of Tel Yoqne'am has pride of place. Drivers waiting for the lights to change probably wonder what the significance of the hill might have been. Excavations by the Hebrew University uncovered the remains of superimposed cities from the Middle Bronze Age, Late Bronze Age and Iron Age periods. The mound has an impressive casemate fortification system from the $10^{th}/9^{th}$ centuries B.C.E., with a street running parallel to the city wall with residential houses. According to the Old Testament the King of Yoqne'am was one of the 31 kings defeated by Joshua (Joshua 12:22; 19:11). Interestingly, in the Crusader period the site was named *Caymont* or *Mons Cain*, because of a tradition that this was the place where Lamech killed Cain.

The ancient mound of Rehov with the white areas indicating the excavation areas. The modern town of Beth Shean can be seen in the distance.

A cylinder seal from Rehov depicting a worshipper.

Rehov

Rehov is a very prominent ancient mound in the Jordan Valley to the south of Beth Shean. The mound is divided into upper and lower parts and from the road it has the appearance "of a large whale rising out of the sea", as one archaeologist digging there aptly described it. Considerable excavations have taken place in recent years but because of the immense size of the site it seems from the air as if the excavators have hardly scratched its surface. The excavations brought to light Late Bronze Age and Iron Age levels, with buildings, fortifications and rich artifacts. The name *Rehov* – derived from a Semitic root indicating a broad or wide space (such as a street) – is a city that was mentioned in the stele of Seti I from Beth Shean and in the city lists of the Egyptian Sheshonq (Shishak). At a short distance from the mound, to the northwest, next to the highway, a synagogue was uncovered dating from the 4th-7th centuries C.E. with an amazing 29-line Hebrew inscription in one of its mosaic floors, the longest ever discovered.

The mound of Yoqne'am next to the modern town.

Megiddo

It is not exactly what one might expect to experience at the site of *Armageddon*, which, according to the Book of Revelation (16:16), is the place where the Kings of the Earth will one day gather to attend the final battle between forces of Evil and the Word of God.

It is difficult to imagine a momentous and overpowering event such as the End of the World, taking place in the placid and lush surroundings of the fertile plain of Jezreel, close to the ancient mound of Megiddo, which, at the time of my visit, was populated by large expanses of wheat billowing serenely in the wind.

The name Armageddon is actually a garbling of the Hebrew word *Har* (meaning "hill" or "mountain") with the name of the ancient city of *Megiddo/Megiddon* known from Scripture (Josh. 17:11; Zech. 12:11). Megiddo, according to Ezekiel (38:8), is the setting for the final conflict between Gog and Magog.

The site was extensively excavated by an American team of archaeologists in numerous campaigns of digging during the 1920s and 1930s, giving the mound a cut-away appearance, and allowing visitors today to descend down to the different historical levels dating principally from the Iron Age and Middle and Early Bronze Ages.

Entering through the area of the city gate, one climbs up the hill, passing the stone pillared buildings, thought by some to be remnants of stables from the time of Solomon, to a lookout point from which one may scan the site and the adjacent valley. In the deep cleft created by excavators one can discern the remains of broad-room temples dating from the Early Bronze Age, with a large stepped round altar evident to one side. Further up the mound is an enormous circular stone-lined pit which was probably a public depot for the storage of grain. The water system, on the other side of the mound, may be approached by descending a steep flight of steps, originally cut along the walls of a vertical rock-cut shaft, giving access to a subterranean horizontal tunnel leading to the place where fresh water wells up. The water system and the site famously inspired James Michener when he was writing his best-selling novel *The Source*.

The site is once again the target of investigation by archaeologists from Tel Aviv University, and in the hot summer months teams of diggers may be seen attacking with gusto the accumulated layers of ancient soil and rubble with pickaxes and shovels held firmly in their hands.

Four decorated ivory objects from the excavations.

The mound of Megiddo and the Plain of Armageddon in the distance. The gaping hole in the foreground is the entrance to a large water-supply system.

"And I saw three unclean spirits like frogs come out of the mouth of the dragon, and out of the mouth of the beast, and out of the mouth of the false prophet… And he gathered them together into a place called in the Hebrew tongue Armageddon" (Revelation 16:13-16)

Samaria and the Jezreel Valley

The hill of Samaria, with the acropolis at the top, and the later columned street leading from a gate with towers below on the left.

The area of the Israelite palace on the acropolis of the city.

Samaria

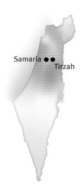

Samaria ● ● Tirzah

King Omri made Samaria the capital city of the Kings of Israel, replacing Tirzah. Omri purchased the hill from a man named Shemer for two talents of silver. According to the Old Testament it was the domicile of the hated Jezebel, the wife of Ahab (871-852 B.C.E.), who was of Phoenician origin.

Archaeological excavations in the 1930s may have brought to light parts of Ahab's "ivory house" (I Kings 22:39; see also the "beds of ivory" mentioned in Amos 6:4) since numerous fragments of ivory plaques which once decorated furnishings were uncovered. Judging by the images carved on these ivory plaques they appear to have been made under Phoenician and Egyptian influences.

At the top of the hill archaeologists brought to light a rectangular walled enclosure containing a large building that might have been the palace of the Kings of Israel.

"I will make Samaria as a heap of the field" (Micah 1:6).

Tirzah

Tirzah was the capital of the northern kingdom of Israel until the time of King Omri (882-871 B.C.E.), who decided to make his capital at Samaria instead (1 Kings 16: 23-24). Tirzah is identified with the site of Tell el-Farah (north), situated not far to the north of Shechem (Nablus). Archaeologists revealed the remains of ancient cities there from the Early Bronze, Middle Bronze and Iron Ages. Because of the way Tirzah was embellished and decorated by the Kings of Israel it was lauded in the Song of Songs (6:4), together with Jerusalem, as a symbol of extreme beauty. The city was laid waste in 732 B.C.E. by the Assyrians.

A view of the French excavations at Tirzah, with the line of the city wall on the left.

"Thou are beautiful, O my love, as Tirzah, comely as Jerusalem, terrible as an army with banners" (Song of Songs 6:4).

Dothan

Perched above a fertile valley not far from Shechem (Nablus), Dothan figures in the story of Joseph who went in search of his brothers as related in the book of Genesis (37: 17); the brothers cruelly threw Joseph into a pit at Dothan. Excavations were made there in the 1950s and 1960s, with the discovery of Early Bronze Age fortifications and Late Bronze Age remains, with gruesome evidence of a mass burial of some 100 individuals within a single tomb. Most of the finds were from the Iron Age, with a street and dwellings containing ovens and storerooms. In an area next to a brick kiln archaeologists found a broken brick with a hoof-print which was evidence of a wandering goat going astray in the brick yard. One of the participants in the excavations at Tel Dothan in the 1960s described the methods and difficulties of digging this site and wrote that a measure of humor and goodwill always helped the excavation along, sometimes even a spot of singing: "One member in our crew started work each day with a song (at least he called it that!)." One of the exciting discoveries at the site was a large multiple-handle Iron Age krater decorated with animals which was found shattered in pieces and then was eventually restored like a jig-saw puzzle into its original shape. This unusual find probably made the excavators sing with joy!

The ancient mound of Dothan with one area of excavations visible.

Jezreel

A joint British-Israeli archaeological excavation was conducted in the 1990s at the site of a mound near the ruined village of Zerin, in the eastern part of the Jezreel Valley. It brought to light a large fortified enclosure dating from the Iron Age surrounded by a dry rock-cut moat. This fortified enclosure may very well have been built by Omri or by Ahab. The site was apparently destroyed in 842 B.C.E. at the end of the reign of Jehoram.

The Iron Age fortifications discovered during excavations at Jezreel, and the appearance of the site in a photograph taken in 1894 (*right*).

"At Dothan we worked in three areas employing about thirty-five men. Two of each crew are trained, one using the pick to dig cautiously when an artifact comes into view, and the other digging under the watchful eye of the supervisor so as not to damage anything with his 'shovel' pick. One 'scoops' the dirt into baskets and the rest carry the dirt to the dump area. Just before the dirt is 'scooped' into the gufa (a basket made from an old rubber tire), the supervisor has made sure that no small object (coin, bead, etc.) has escaped."

(Robert T. Boyd, A Pictorial Guide to Biblical Archaeology, 1969, p. 44)

Top: a multi-handled large krater from the Iron Age decorated with animals, found at Dothan. *Bottom:* a decorated cultic stand from Taanach and (*right*) one of the excavation areas with impressive ancient building remains.

Taanach

Situated near the southern end of the Jezreel Valley, near the Wadi Ara pass, Taanach (Arabic Ti'inik) is a site which produced a rich array of archaeological remains, including a number of very important cuneiform tablets. With continued Israelite extension of territory from the time of Joshua, the Bible tells us that Taanach succeeded in remaining in Canaanite hands until the crucial battle of Deborah and Barak "at Taanach" (Judges 5:19).

A wonderful cultic ceramic stand from the early Iron Age was found at the site decorated with tiers of lions and mythical creatures.

57

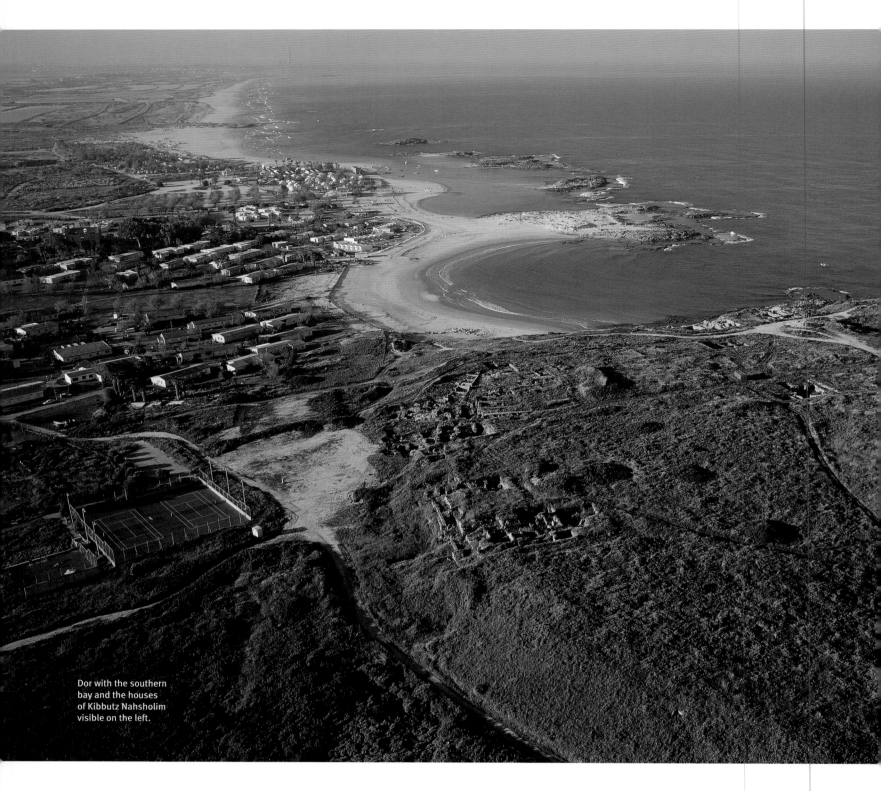

Dor with the southern
bay and the houses
of Kibbutz Nahsholim
visible on the left.

Dor

When Corporal Henry Phillips arrived at the site
in 1866 he was able to record by photography a
very tall tower standing at one end of the large
mound of Tel Dor (Tanturah; Khirbet el-Burj)
and overlooking the Mediterranean sea. Today,
the tower, a remnant of the Crusader fort *Merle*,
has collapsed into a pile of rubble and cement
and is no longer a significant landmark. However,
archaeologists, working in the early 1920s,
and more recently since 1980, with teams from the Hebrew
University, were not really interested in the Crusader remains

but have been looking for much earlier archaeological remains
within the large 30-acre mound and especially for tantalizing
traces of the northern "Sea People", such as the *Šikila / Tjekker*,
who are said to have occupied Dor (*Duru*) and other parts of the
Sharon Plain in the early 12th century B.C.E. They have been
successful, but they have had to dig through many superimposed
layers from the later Persian, Hellenistic and Roman periods. In
the description of the Egyptian seafarer Wenamon's voyage to the
Carmel Coast and Phoenicia in around the year 1070 B.C.E., he
describes his ship docking at Dor and subsequently his anguish
over having been robbed of his gold and silver.

"…until recently hardly any tangible archaeological evidence for northern 'Sea People' has been forthcoming. As a result, nearly all general studies concerning 'Sea People' in the Levant concentrate almost exclusively on the Philistines, mentioning the others only in passing…"

(Ayelet Gilboa, "Sea Peoples and Phoenicians along the Southern Phoenician Coast" Bulletin of the American Schools of Oriental Research 337, 2005, p. 49).

One of the excavation areas with Persian and Hellenistic fortification walls, and (*below*) a ceramic vessel from the dig with the features of an African man.

The journey of Wenamon: "I reached Dor, a town of the Tjekker, and Beder, its prince, had 50 loaves of bread, one jug of wine, and one leg of beef brought to me. And a man of my ship ran away and stole one [vessel] of gold, [amounting] to 5 deben, four jars of silver, amounting to 20 deben, and a sack of 11 deben of silver… I got up in the morning, and I went to the place where the Prince was, and I said to him: 'I have been robbed in your harbor. Now you are prince of this land, and you are its investigator who should look for my silver… And he said to me: 'Whether you are important or whether you are eminent – look here, I do not recognize this accusation which you have made to me! Suppose it had been a thief who belonged to my land who went on your boat and stole your silver, I should have repaid it to you from my treasury, until they had found this thief of yours – whoever he may be. Now about the thief who robbed you – he belongs to you! He belongs to your ship! Spend a few days here visiting me, so that I may look for him.'" (J. B. Pritchard, ed., The Ancient Near East. Vol. I: An Anthology of Text and Pictures. 1973, pp. 17-18)

The six-line Siloam inscription now in the Istanbul Museum (*left*) and inscribed seal impressions from the City of David excavations (*above*).

Jerusalem and the City of David

The earlier city of Jerusalem was situated on an unimposing hill (later known as the "City of David") with a bubbling spring of fresh water (the Gichon Spring) at its eastern foot. Jerusalem has its origins way back in the Neolithic period, with people being drawn to the place because of its copious source of water. Subsequently, in the Middle Bronze Age, the spring itself was heavily protected and surrounded by massive towers built of enormous slabs of stone. It must have been an impressive view, when approaching Jerusalem, to see below the small town, a citadel of lofty towers enclosing the main water source. These fortifications were apparently in ruins when, according to the Bible, King David, and his faithful Captain Joab, are said to have approached the town with the intention of conquering it from the Jebusites. Perhaps the Jebusites restored the upper parts of these earlier towers and it may therefore have been these that were partly scaled by David, notwithstanding the taunts of the lame and the disabled made by those in the town above (II Samuel 5: 6-9). Jerusalem subsequently became the

capital of Israel, with a Temple to God on Mount Moriah, which was built by Solomon (I Kings 6). A large building has recently been excavated on the northern part of the City of David ridge and identified as that of the Royal Palace.

In the 8th century B.C.E., at the time of King Hezekiah, the city was strongly re-fortified in view of the approach of the Assyrian army of Sennacherib. Massive fortifications – notably the "broad wall" in the Jewish Quarter – have been uncovered, and these were in use until the destruction of the city in 587/586 B.C.E. Sennacherib's siege of the city in 701 B.C.E. was not a success (II Kings 18: 13; 19). Substantial work was also done on the water system at the time of King Hezekiah (II Kings 20:20 and II Chronicles 32:30) and this has been confirmed by the discovery in August 1880 of the Siloam Inscription in the rock wall of a water tunnel to the south of the Temple Mount in Jerusalem. A number of important artifacts have been found in Jerusalem and its vicinity, which shed light on the city and its inhabitants in the years leading up to the destruction of the city and its Temple in 586/587 B.C.E. at the hands of Nebuchadnezzar, the Babylonian king. Within a rock-hewn tomb at Ketef

Hinnom, on the west side of the city, two silver scrolls (which at the time of the discovery looked like abandoned cigarette buts) turned out, when unraveled, to be amulets inscribed with the Priestly Benediction (Numbers 6: 24-26). Scattered on the east slope of the City of David, amidst the rubble and destruction caused by the Babylonians, archaeologists found a group of 51 seal impressions (*bullae*), some of which include Hebrew names, such as Gemaryahu son of Shaphan", who may, incredibly, be identical to a scribe who was active in the court of Jehoiakim in the fifth year of his reign in 604 B.C.E. (Jeremiah 36: 9-12), about eighteen years before the destruction of the city.

The stepped-stone structure in the City of David with the remains of a possible palace from the 10th century B.C.E. on the ridge above.

The City of David from the south with the Siloam Pool in the foreground (before it was excavated, see page 91)

Two artifacts from the Iron Age: a scepter head shaped like a pomegranate, from Motza, outside Jerusalem *(top)*, and a silver scroll inscribed with the Priestly Benediction from a tomb in Ketef Hinnom, immediately west of the city *(below)*.

The Siloam inscription: "[…when] (the tunnel) was driven through. And this was the way in which it was cut through: – While […] (were) still […] axe(s), each man toward his fellow, and while there were still three cubits to be cut through [there was heard] the voice of a man calling to his fellow, for there was an overlap in the rock on the right [and on the left]. And when the tunnel was driven through, the quarrymen hewed (the rock), each man toward his fellow, axe against axe; and the water flowed from the spring toward the reservoir for 1,200 cubits, and the height of the rock above the head(s) of the quarrymen was 100 cubits." (J. B. Pritchard, ed., The Ancient Near East. Vol. I: An

Anthology of Text and Pictures. 1973, pp. 212)

The large mound of Lachish, with the adjacent moshav beyond.

Lachish

An amazing discovery of eighteen inscribed potsherds (*ostraca*) was made in 1936 by an archaeological team working at Tell ed-Duweir (identified as Lachish) headed by James Leslie Starkey, while clearing out the burnt rooms of the gatehouse on the south-west side of the ancient mound. These Hebrew inscribed *ostraca* – now known as the "Lachish Letters" – were written by a subordinate and addressed to "my lord Yaush", who was apparently the city commander of Lachish, not long before the destruction of the city by Babylonians in 587/586 B.C.E. The subordinate, it would appear, wrote the letters while stationed at a location where he could watch for signals from both Lachish and Azekah, perhaps at Maresha.

Starkey met a tragic end when he was murdered in January 1938 on his way to Jerusalem to attend the official opening of the Palestine Archaeological Museum (now the Rockefeller Museum).

Lachish was subsequently excavated by a team of archaeologists from the Tel Aviv University, discovering remains from the Middle and Late Bronze Ages, and excavating substantial Iron Age remains, including a palace-fort. Since the Iron Age city had been destroyed twice, once by the Assyrians in 701 B.C.E. and then again by the Babylonians in 587/586 B.C.E., the detailed investigation of the material culture from these two separate levels in the mound (Levels III and II) have been enormously important for archaeologists working on Iron Age remains elsewhere in the country.

An early photograph of the British archaeologist J.L. Starkey indicating with his walking stick the exact spot at the gateway where the famous Lachish letters were found.

View of the mound of Azekah, a city located not very far away from Lachish, which was also destroyed by the Babylonians.

Lachish Letter IV: "And [my lord] will know that we are watching for the signals of Lachish, according to all the signs for which my lord have given, for we cannot see Azekah." (O. Tufnell, "Lachish", in D. Winton Thomas ed., Archaeology and Old Testament Study, 1967, page 306).

Some of the famous Lachish letters inscribed on potsherds (*ostraca*).

The gateway in which the Lachish letters were found.

Cities of Benjamin

Although the territory of the Tribe of Benjamin was relatively small it played an important role in the unification of the other tribes during the period of the Judges. Very specifically Saul, a Benjamite, became the first king of Israel (Judges 3:15; I Samuel 9:16-17) and was seen to be a deliverer from Philistine oppression. However, the episode of the murder of the concubine of the Levite at Gibeah (identified as Tell el-Ful), prompted extreme animosity from the other tribes, and the inhabitants of Gibeah were all put to the sword.

The sprawling village of Jabaʼ which has scattered archaeological remains from different periods, and (*below*) archaeological excavations on the east slope of Tell el-Ful.

Gibeah and Jabaʻ

Tell el-Ful (Arabic for "hill of the horsebeans") is a sorry looking hill, encroached on three of its sides by the houses of the village of Shuʻfat and on its fourth side by the modern Jerusalem neighborhood of Pisgat Zeev. On top of the hill is the abandoned cement shell of a building that was designed in 1965 to serve as a new palace for the Hashemite King Hussein of Jordan. However, the Six-Day war in 1967 put an end to progress on this construction.

The well-known American archaeologist, philologist and scholar, W.F. Albright, excavated the summit of the hill in the 1920s, revealing the remains of a tower dating back to the Early Iron Age. He believed that the site should be identified as Saul's hometown Gibeah (I Samuel 10: 26; 11:4). Further excavations were conducted in the mid-1960s, to make way for the construction of Hussein's palace, and in the mid-1990s on its eastern slopes by the Israel Antiquities Authority, revealing significant remains of Middle Bronze Age and Roman settlements.

Jabaʻ is a village situated to the north-east of the promontory of er-Ram. Some have suggested that it should be identified as Gibeah instead of Tel el-Ful. This, however, seems unlikely since Jabaʻ is on the whole a medieval village which was rebuilt in the Ottoman period. The few scattered Iron Age potsherds that have been found at the site are unlikely to change the identification of Gibeah to this location.

Top and bottom: the water system with spiral steps at El-Jib (Gibeon).

Gibeon

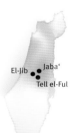

El-Jib • • Jaba'
• Tell el-Ful

Next to the modern village of el-Jib to the northwest of Jerusalem is a hill covered with ancient remains which is identified as ancient Gibeon. Excavations were conducted there by an American expedition in the late 1950s and early 1960s, with the discovery of Iron Age remains, including fortifications, dwellings, caves and an elaborate water system with a large rock-cut circular pool (11 meters in diameter and 25 meters deep) and with a flight of 79 steps leading down to its bottom. It may be the same pool as the one referred to in II Samuel (2:13-16): "And Joab the son of Zeruiah, and the servants of David, went out, and met together by the pool of Gibeon; and they sat down, the one on the one side of the pool, and the other on the other side of the pool. And Abner said to Joab, Let the young men now arise, and play before us. And Joab said, Let them arise… And they caught every one his fellow by the head, and thrust his sword in his fellow's side; so they fell down together: wherefore that place was called Helkath-hazzurim, which is in Gibeon."

"Then spake Joshua to the Lord in the day when the Lord delivered up the Amorites before the Children of Israel, and he said in the sight of Israel, 'Sun, stand thou still upon Gibeon; and thou, Moon, in the Valley of Ajalon.' And the sun stood still, and the moon stayed, until the people had avenged themselves upon their enemies." (Joshua 10: 12-13)

Beersheba

Beersheba is a place connected with the making of covenants in the biblical tradition. When the King of nearby Gerar seized a well that belonged to the Patriarch Abraham, a covenant was eventually struck between the contestants on oath (*shebuah* in Hebrew), and from that moment on the place was called Beersheba, the "well of the oath" (Genesis 21: 22-22-23). Isaac also concluded a covenant at Beersheba and dug a well there. Beersheba became an important religious and administrative center in the south of the country in the first millennium B.C.E. and it would seem that the saying "from Dan [situated in the far north] to Beersheba" reflects this (Judges 20:1).

Archaeologists seem certain that they have identified biblical Beersheba at the site of the mound of Tell es-Seba (Tel Sheva), situated not far to the east of the modern town. Excavations revealed a fortified Israelite city with an oval urban layout, with streets, houses and storehouses, as well as a major subterranean water system.

Exploration in the Negev Desert in the 1950s: "This was the era of hard-desert living, when we camped under the open starry sky. Many of us grew beards during the trips and on our return to Beer Sheba we would look like gun-packing frontiersmen from the Wild West" (M. Evenari, L. Shanan and N. Tadmor, The Negev: The Challenge of a Desert. 1971, p. 1)

The traditional well of Abraham in a photograph taken in 1875. *Right:* the biblical city of Beersheba after excavation and reconstruction. *Bottom:* one of the buildings excavated within the ancient city.

"Paths from all directions and people of most diverse backgrounds and culture have met in Beer Sheba from the start of the story of civilization. Its position, wells, soil and constantly renewed population have given it a deserved pre-eminence in the memories and annals of history." (N. Glueck, Rivers in the Desert: A History of the Negev. 1959, page 41).

Colonel S.F. Newcombe recalled meeting in January 1914 with T.E. Lawrence (of Arabia) and Leonard Woolley who made an archaeological survey of the area: "Arriving in Beer Sheba I found Leonard Woolley and Lawrence… It gave me rather a shock to find such young people taking on the job. However, I soon found they were very much alive indeed, and we spent the next few days together, in which they told me all the biblical and archaeological history of the southern desert. I had read many books on the area but they were very much out of date and based on supposition and theory; hence it was a great relief to talk on the spot with two people who had very sound ideas on archaeology, and they gave me a very reasonable idea of what had happened. And it was intensely interesting for us because we were working in the country with people who were probably wearing the same kind of clothes and eating about the same kind of food – and that is not much, anyway – and going without washing and water much as the Israelites had done." (S.F. Newcombe, Palestine Exploration Fund Quarterly Statement, October 1935, p. 162)

Beit Mirsim

Despite the actions of various landowners to extract as much money as they could out of the excavator of the site, W.F. Albright, during his campaigns of 1926-32, nobody was discouraged and the archaeological finds that were eventually made there during the digging operations were very important for the development of archaeology in the Land of Israel. The hill of Tell Beit Mirsim, which Albright thought might be biblical Debir (Joshua 15: 49), is situated to the south-west of Hebron.

The layout of the Iron Age city was revealed during the digging and much pottery and other finds were methodically recorded. It was exciting, Albright recalled in 1949, to excavate a town dating from biblical times: "…the plans and contents of scores of houses have been published and give, for the first time, a clear picture of the way in which the people of Judah lived at the time of Isaiah and Jeremiah."

Albright was unable to locate the cemetery of the site, writing: "…strange to say, no native seems to have any idea where the ancient cemeteries of Tell Beit Mirsim were located and not a tomb appears to have been opened and robbed." In the late 1970s, however, the ancient cemetery of Tell Beit Mirsim was discovered and systematically looted by robbers, and it took a concerted plan of action by the Israeli authorities to excavate and plot the rock-cut tombs and to record the finds for posterity.

Top: general view of the mound with its cemetery in the foreground. *Bottom:* a limestone libation tray from the Iron Age decorated with the image of a lion.

Edomite Sites

Anybody watching the main roads leading into the southern part of the country from across the Arabah Desert in the east in the late 7th or early 6th centuries B.C.E., might have been able to see a constant flow of groups of people, with their animals and goods transported on wagons, moving from one water source to another. These newcomers were the Edomites and eventually they firmly established themselves in the territory, later known as Idumaea, to the south of the Kingdom of Judah.

Unlike the Israelites, who shied away from depicting themselves on artistic objects and were forbidden from depicting their God, the Edomites had no qualms whatsoever in creating figurines and statuettes, especially of cultic significance and many of them are of great beauty. At Horvat Qitmit, not far to the south of Arad, archaeologists uncovered a 7th century B.C.E. shrine with a *bema* (cultic platform) and a large number of ceramic figurines, statues, reliefs, stands and cultic vessels.

In recent years an amazing discovery was made of a shrine with an enormous cache of 67 figurines, stands and vessels at Ein Husb (Mezad Hatzeva), situated on an important cross-road in the Arabah, on the north-south road leading towards the Gulf of Eilat, and on the east-west road linking Transjordan with the Negev Desert. The site has been identified with biblical Tamar, the city of palm trees (Judges 1:16). Idols, such as the ones found at Hatzeva, may have led to the religious reform of King Josiah (640-609 B.C.E.) in which he commanded that the priests "bring forth out of the temple of the Lord *all the vessels* that were made for Baal, and for the grove [of Asherah], and for all the host of the heaven: and he burned them…" (II Kings 23: 4).

A horned deity from Qitmit (*right*) and two human-formed cultic stands from Hatzeva (*below*).

"The south side [of the border], towards the south, shall be from Tamar to the waters of Meribah by Kadesh, along the brook to the Great Sea." (Ezekiel 47: 19).

View of the excavations in progress at Hatzeva. A *favissa* of cultic stands and other rare Edomite objects were found at the site.

Top: two iron age inscribed potsherds from the site. *Bottom*: the Citadel in spring time.

Arad

One of the excavators of the ancient site of Arad, Ruth Amiran, who resided in Jerusalem, wrote a postcard to me during the peak of one of the winters in the early 1970s, when I was living in the nearby modern town of Arad: "Dear Shimon. It is snowing here in Jerusalem. Is it snowing there in Arad? Ruth". The answer is that it was, but the phenomenon of snow in the desert is a rare and a wondrous sight to behold, as I can rightly testify. Swathes of snow fill the wadis and extend in tantalizing shapes along the glistening slopes of hills, delineating the paths made by the wandering goats making them appear as miniature terraces. The glare from the snow is almost impossible to bear.

The Israelite royal citadel, looming above the ruins of the Canaanite city, was excavated by another archaeologist, Yohanan Aharoni of Tel Aviv University. Excavations were able to show that during the period of the Monarchy the site was destroyed and burnt at least six times; it was a wonder that anybody ever wanted to come back to live there. Perhaps one reason was that this was the traditional "high place" of the venerated Kenite family (Judges 1:16). A temple with standing stones was found in the north-west corner of the Citadel. More than 200 inscribed potsherds were found, written in Hebrew and Aramaic. Some of the later examples came from the archive of an official named Eliashib son of Eshyahu. One of the *ostraca* refers to the "House of Yahweh" and this is presumably a direct reference to the Temple of God in Jerusalem.

The Iron Age citadel at
Arad after a fall of snow.

Part Three:

IMPACT OF THE GREEK AND ROMAN WORLDS

"Soon Hellenized native cities sprang up all over the Seleucid kingdom. Educated natives, particularly in the western provinces, made every effort to assimilate themselves to the ruling class. Cities and individuals adopted Hellenized names and invented claims to Greek or at least Trojan ancestry; and local gods were equated with members of the Greek pantheon. A Jew called Joshua could become Jason, and the Jewish God, became, to many, Olympian Zeus." (E. Badian, "The Hellenistic World", in H. Lloyd-Jones, ed., The Greek World. 1962, page 250).

With the advent of the Hellenistic period the main political and cultural influences on the people of the country came from the Greek and Roman worlds. The Greek era began in 332 B.C.E. when Alexander the Great defeated the King of Persia at the Battle of Issus, thereby opening up the way for the conquest of Syria and Palestine. After Alexander's death, his kingdom was divided among his generals and the country was controlled either by the Egyptian-based Ptolemids or the Syrian-based Seleucids.

Hellenization as a process of cultural unification, as perceived by Alexander and his successors, did not however have the full desired effect in Palestine where local Jewish nationalism, for example, found itself actually boosted by the external pressures of the Hellenization process, ultimately leading to the Maccabean Revolt. The Roman influence in the country began with the conquest of Palestine by Pompey in 63 B.C.E. and later actually increased under Herod the Great, who is known to have built a Greek theater, an amphitheater where Jews wrestled naked with Greeks, and a hippodrome close to Jerusalem.

A bronze head of Hadrian
found at Shalem

A view of the mound of Shikmona on the Mediterranean coast, just south of the modern city of Haifa. The remains of a large ancient building are visible in the foreground.

Shikmona, Michal and Nahal Teninim

Phoenician influence was very strong in the north of the country, notwithstanding the fact that their cultural center was situated within the coastal area of Lebanon. Phoenician influence spread southwards along the Mediterranean coast, from Tel Shikmona, near Haifa, down to Tel Michal in the southern Sharon Plain. Both sites had thriving Persian and Hellenistic settlements, which derived their wealth primarily because of their proximity to the sea and their ports, on the one hand, as well as to the trading opportunities connected to the main highway, the *Via Maris*, which extended north-south along the coast, on the other. Some of the rich statuary and figurines from Tel Michal, for instance, attest to the high standard of living that its inhabitants enjoyed.

Left: the ancient mound of Michal and the adjacent marina under construction, and (*top and right*) three figurines from the site.

Anafa

At Tel Anafa in the Upper Galilee archaeologists brought to light a group of buildings and artifacts that reflect the wealthy lifestyle of a group of Hellenized Phoenicians. Houses were impressively decorated with paneled walls, some covered with gold-leaf and others richly-painted, and floors were paved with mosaics. One of the buildings contained a bath and this is probably the oldest heated bath hitherto found in Palestine. Fragments of tens of thousands of glass vessels were found in the excavation, this from a time when glass was a rare commodity. Clearly, the inhabitants at Tel Anafa had a very enjoyable life, but everything came to an end when the settlement was abandoned around 75 B.C.E.

Top: the Hellenistic site of Anafa. *Bottom*: the excavation of a water system and aqueduct in Nahal Teninim.

Mount Gerizim

The temple of the Samaritans was situated on the summit of Mount Gerizim near Shechem (Nablus). In its heyday (circa 332 B.C.E.) it must have been a magnificent sight to behold, with steps leading up to a broad esplanade on which the temple soared to the sky, glinting in the sun.

Archaeological excavations have been conducted since 1983 around the Byzantine church (the Church of Mary the Theodokos built by emperor Zeno in 484 C.E.), revealing a monumental temple enclosure dating from the Hellenistic period, with earlier remains going back to the Iron Age. Large buildings and houses from the Hellenistic period have also been uncovered, surrounded by a fortification wall with gates. 480 inscriptions were dug up written mainly in Aramaic, with a few in Hebrew and Greek. The Samaritans consider themselves to be the true followers of the ancient Israelite line and their Torah (the *Samaritikon*) dates to the time of Moses. Today only a dwindling number of Samaritans live and worship at the site.

Top: view of excavations on the summit of Mount Gerizim after a fall of snow. The main square building is of Byzantine date, but the underlying walls in the foreground date from the Persian and Hellenistic periods. *Left*: another view of the Mount Gerizim summit with Mount Ebal on the horizon. *Right*: a fragment of a Samaritan dedicatory inscription found in the excavations.

"And it shall come to pass, when the Lord thy God hath brought thee in unto the Land whither thou goest to possess it, that thou shalt put the blessing upon Mount Gerizim, and the curse upon Mount Ebal"

(Deuterononomy 11:29)

A Samaritan dedicatory inscription (dated 150-50 B.C.E.) found on the Greek island of Delos: "The Israelites on Delos who make first-fruit offerings to Holy Argarizin [Har Gerizim] crown with a golden crown Sarapion son of Jason of Knossos for his benefactions on their behalf".

Maresha (Marissa)

Maresha is an Idumean city surrounded by a myriad of subterranean caves. Some of these caves have highly complex plans with convoluted chambers, winding passages and rock-cut flights of steps descending into the murky depths of the ground. Mystery has been wrapped around many of these caves ever since they were first explored in the nineteenth century, but recent work has shown that quite a few of them had straightforward mundane functions: as storage areas, underground oil presses and stables. Further afield are caves that were definitely used for burial purposes, of which the most spectacular is a painted tomb in the eastern cemetery with an inscription mentioning members of the Sidonian community

A wall painting with a depiction of an elephant and Greek inscriptions, that was discovered in a Hellenistic tomb for Sidonians at Maresha.

"residing at Marissa" in the Hellenistic period. On the walls of this tomb are depictions of thirteen types of animals, including an elephant and mythical creatures, notably Cerebus the three-headed watchdog of Hades, as well as wreaths, human figures and Greek inscriptions.

African elephants (Elephas africanus) *were employed by Darius in his battle against Alexander the Great. They were introduced into the Land of Israel by the Syrian-Greek army for military purposes in battle (1 Macc. 8:6; 2 Macc. 13:15) and it was under one of them that Eleazar the Hasmonean was crushed to death (I Macc. 6:43–46). According to Jewish custom on seeing an elephant one should recite the blessing: "Blessed is He who makes strange creatures"* (Ber. 58b).

A large cave which was used as a columbarium (dovecote) in Hellenistic times. *Opposite*: the upper city or acropolis of Maresha, with the recent excavations of a corner tower visible in the center of the picture.

"Eleazar also, surnamed Savaran, perceived that one of the beasts [an elephant], armed with royal harness, was higher than all the rest, and supposing that the king was upon him, put himself in jeopardy, to the end he might deliver his people, and get him a perpetual name. Whereupon he ran upon him courageously through the midst of the battle, slaying on the right hand side and on the left, so that they were divided from him on both sides. Which done, he crept under the elephant, and thrust him under, and slew him; whereupon the elephant fell down upon him and there he died."

(I Maccabees 6: 43-46).

81

Searching for Modi'in of the Maccabees

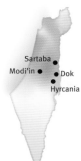

The whereabouts of Modi'in, the town and burial-place of the Maccabean family, is a mystery that has intrigued scholars since the nineteenth century. According to I Maccabees (13: 25-30) Josephus (Antiq. XIII, 211), the burial-place built by Simon the Hasmonean at Modi'in was extremely elaborate and boasted seven pyramids. Such a site should have been visible for some distance. The archbishop of Caesarea, Eusebius Pamphili (c. 260-339 C.E.) indicated that the burial-place of the Maccabees was still to be seen in his day (*Onom.* 132:16), and its position was also clearly marked on the well-known Madaba mosaic map (mid-sixth century). But the exact location of Modi'in was forgotten in medieval times. In the twelfth century the Crusaders mistakenly identified it at the site of Belmont, next to Kibbutz Tsuba of today, west of Jerusalem, and this confusion was maintained until the nineteenth century by some travelers to the region.

In the mid-nineteenth century numerous efforts were made by scholars to identify Modi'in at Khirbet el-Midya in the northern Shephelah, but the famous "Tombs of the Maccabees" that may be seen there today are mostly of Byzantine date. In recent years proposals have been put forward to identify ancient Modi'in at Horvat Titura (Khirbet el-Burj), which was a large central settlement, or at Khirbet Umm el-'Umdan, which is the site of an Early Roman period village, with a public building (perhaps a synagogue). But the mystery remains…

Bottom: the so-called "Tombs of the Maccabees" at Khirbet el-Midya. *Top*: a recently excavated synagogue from the 1st century C.E. at Khirbet Umm el-'Umdan.

"Then sent Simon, and took the bones of Jonathan his brother, and buried them in Modi'in, the city of his fathers. And all Israel made great lamentation for him, and bewailed him many days. Simon also built a monument upon the sepulcher of his father and his brethren, and raised it aloft to the sight, with hewn stone behind and before. Moreover he set up seven pyramids, one against another, for his father and his mother, and his four brethren. And in these he made cunning devices, about the which he set great pillars, and upon the pillars he made all their armour for a perpetual memory, and by the armour ships carved, that they may be seen of all that sail on the sea. This is the sepulcher which he made at Modi'in and it standeth unto this day." (I Maccabees 13: 25-30).

The fortress of Dok with a later enclosure wall and chapel on the summit, with a view of the Jordan Valley in the background.

Hasmonean Fortresses

The Hasmonean kingdom was extremely powerful during its peak years; by the time of Alexander Jannaeus (103-76 B.C.E.) it maintained a vast territory on both sides of the Jordan River. Like other Hellenistic monarchs, the Hasmoneans protected their kingdom by fortifying towns and by setting up fortresses along the edges of their kingdom and at vulnerable locations. The connection between the desert and Hasmoneans was a strong one, going back to the time of the Maccabean Revolt:

"But Judas Maccabeaus with nine others, or thereabout, withdrew himself into the wilderness, and lived in the mountains after the manner of beasts, with his company, who fed on herbs continually, lest they should be partakers of the pollution." (II Maccabees 5:27). Examples of desert fortresses include Sartaba (Alexandrion), Ras Karantal (Dok) and Hyrcania, as well as at Beth Basi which is situated in the desert to the east of Bethlehem.

Hyrcania with the remains of an aqueduct in the foreground. *Right*: the dome-shaped summit of Sartaba. Note the opening to a cistern on its slope.

At the bottom of the hill of Hyrcania in Wadi Sececa are two mysterious rock-cut tunnels with steps descending into the ground. Archaeologists have been patiently digging in these tunnels, clearing one of them to a depth of at least 160 meters, but finding almost no ancient artifacts and without its end in sight. The purpose of these tunnels is unknown and they are unique. Like a good fairy tale, it would be nice to think that locked inside a chamber at the bottom of one of these tunnels is a treasure trove, perhaps the one that Queen Salome Alexandra is said to have stored at Hyrcania, according to the writings of the Jewish historian Josephus Flavius (Antiquities 13: 417), but, unfortunately, in my experience, fairy tales hardly ever come true. But we can still dream…

"Afterward Jonathan, and Simon, and they that were with him, got them away to Bethbasi, which is in the wilderness, and they repaired the decays [of the defenses] thereof, and made it strong. Which thing when [the Greek] Bacchides knew, he gathered together all his host, and sent word to them that were of Judea. Then went he and laid siege against Bethbasi; and they fought against it a long season, and made engines of war." (1 Maccabees 9: 62-64).

Top: the Temple Mount (Haram al-Sharif) seen from the southwest, with the Dome of the Rock on the platform, and with the Jewish place of prayer along the western wall in the lower left of the picture. *Bottom*: Jewish prayer taking place next to the remnant of the Temple Mount wall, known in Hebrew as the *kotel*, built of very large dressed stones from the time of Herod.

The Gaon Achai Shabcha: "Why did the First Temple fall? Because of idolatry, luxury and murder. And why did the Second Temple fall, since we know that in its time the Torah was observed, good works were practiced, and the commandments were respected? It fell because of the unjustified hatreds which reigned then, from which it may be concluded that unjustified hatred is a sin as heavy as idolatry, luxury and murder."

(M. Grindea, ed., *Jerusalem: The Holy Land in Literature*, 1968, p. 49).

Jerusalem at the Time of Herod

An inscription from the parapet of the Temple Mount bearing the inscription "To the Place of the Trumpeting..." (*left*), and a fragmentary Greek inscription from the fence of the inner court of the Jewish Temple (*right*). *Bottom*: the Citadel with the large tower (Hippicus) built by Herod the Great.

Temple and Palace

Endless are the legends and stories woven around the city of Jerusalem which glows within mists of antiquity. In the words of the Hebrew writer Abraham Shlonski: "Jerusalem is a hill city/ the hills are founded on gold and pinnacled with gold/ for among them walked men who saw God." The sanctity of Mount Moriah may be traced back in biblical tradition to the time King David bought the site of a threshing floor from Araunah the Jebusite for the purpose of building an altar to the Israelite God; eventually his son Solomon had a temple constructed at the very spot. The temple building and its surroundings witnessed many changes, leading up to its destruction at the hands of the Babylonians in 597/586 B.C.E. and its rebuilding following the return from Exile. Archaeological finds of these earlier periods have not yet come to light, except for a few artifacts and a few subterranean spaces. What one can see, however, are some remains belonging to the later Second Temple period, notably a section of the western enclosure wall of the Temple Mount which was the focus of prayer for Jews for centuries and was described as the "Wailing Wall" by Western visitors in the nineteenth century.

Herod the Great embarked upon a major remodeling of the Jewish Temple in the centre of the massive level platform in about 22 or

A general view of the magnificent Temple Mount from the south, showing the Muslim buildings on its summit, and extensive archaeological excavations at its foot.

An olive tree along the western Old City wall. Herod's palace (later the Praetorium) was situated behind this wall in the area of the present-day Armenian Garden.

20 B.C.E. The Temple Mount itself was undoubtedly one of the marvels of the Age of Augustus. The construction of the Temple lasted forty-six years, according to the Gospel of John (2: 20). The Temple Mount itself, however, judging by archaeological finds, was apparently still incomplete when the entire city was put to the torch by Titus and the Romans in 70 C.E. Two Greek inscriptions are known which were originally placed on a screen separating the inner and outer courts of the Temple warning Gentiles against entering into the Inner Court. Significant Herodian remains of the areas to the south and southwest of the Temple Mount have been

A wall painting of the top of an arcade with a bird aloft, dating from the 1st century C.E., found in the remains of a house located to the south of Herod's palace on Mount Zion.

uncovered in excavations since 1968, including the impressive substructure for an arched flight of steps leading up to the Royal Stoa above Robinson's Arch. A stone inscribed in Hebrew "to the place of the trumpeting..." was discovered in the debris below the Temple Mount. To the south on the end of the eastern edge of the Ophel a dedicatory Greek inscription was found from the first century – the Theodotos Inscription – referring to a synagogue which was used as a place for "the reading of the Law and for the teaching of the commandments".

In addition to Herod's remarkable building projects within Jerusalem, he also built an enormous palace in the area of the Upper City (within the Jaffa Gate and Armenian Garden parts of today). The palace was protected to the north-west by three monumental towers – Hippicus, Phasael and Mariamne – and consisted of twin buildings and with a sprawling formal garden with fountains and trees to the south. It was most certainly a sight for sore eyes, judging by the detailed description of the palace in the writings of the first-century historian Josephus Flavius, in which he stated emphatically that in "extravagance and equipment no building surpassed it." (Jewish War V, 176-181).

A fragment of a carved stone that once decorated the Royal Stoa situated at the southern end of the Temple Mount (*above*), and the Theodotos Inscription (*left*).

"The physical building may no longer exist, but both the site of the Temple and the idea of it have inspired men and women for generations – and have been fought over with matching intensity. The Temple takes shape in the minds of men. And there's the rub. The Temple is never just a destroyed building. It has become the most potent symbol of the human search for a lost ideal, an image of former greatness and greatness to come. It is an idea that has prompted struggle, brutal war between cultures and nations, and some of the most moving poetry and art of the Western tradition." (Simon Goldhill, The Temple of Jerusalem, 2005, p. 7).

Translation of the Greek Theodotos inscription from Jerusalem:
"Theodotus son of Vettenus, priest and archisynagogos, son of an archisynagogos and grandson of an archisynagogos, built the assembly hall (synagoge) for the reading of the Law and for the teaching of the commandments, and the guest room, the chambers, and the water fittings, as an inn for those in need from foreign parts, [the synagogue] which his fathers founded with the elders and Simonides." (J. S. Kloppenborg, "The Theodotos Inscription from Jerusalem and the Problem of First-Century Synagogue Buildings", in J. Charlesworth ed., Jesus and Archaeology, 2006, pp. 252-253).

The *menorah* and shewbread table of the Temple incised into plaster, found during excavations in the Jewish Quarter in Jerusalem.

Pools: Bethesda and Siloam

Maintaining a state of purity was paramount in the minds of the Jewish inhabitants of Jerusalem in the decades preceding the destruction of the city in 70 C.E. Many stone vessels – carved mugs and large jars which were used for hand-washing rituals – have been found within houses excavated by archaeologists in different parts of the city. Also many water purification pools (*mikva'ot*) used for ritual bathing have been uncovered, but these would certainly not have not sufficed for the needs of the many thousands of pilgrims who flocked to the city during festival times to worship at the holiest of sites, namely the House of God (the Jewish Temple). Hence, the Siloam and Bethesda Pools were designed, probably at the time of Herod the Great, to accommodate almost all the purification needs of the many Jewish festival-goers to Jerusalem. Archaeological finds at both sites show that the pools have flights of steps with intermittent landings to facilitate bathing procedures. Healing accounts associated with Jesus are connected to both these pools: the story of the miracle of the blind man regaining his sight at the Siloam Pool (John 9: 7, 11) and the healing of an infirm man at the Bethesda Pool (John 5: 2-9).

The area of the Bethesda Pool with the remains of a house from the 1st century C.E. in the foreground. The medieval Probatica Chapel is visible behind. *Bottom*: Byzantine inscription from the Bethesda Pool excavations.

"Now there is at Jerusalem by the sheep market a pool, which is called in the Hebrew tongue Bethesda, having five porches. In these lay a great number of impotent folk, of blind, halt, withered, waiting for the moving of the water. For an angel went down at a certain season into the pool, and troubled the water: whosoever then first after the troubling of the water stepped in was made whole of whatsoever disease he had." (John 5: 2-4).

Top and bottom: the Siloam Pool excavations showing the steps and landings.

The medieval Church of St Anne, with the Bethesda Pool excavations visible on the left.

"*Jasmin blossoms surrounded the Pool of Siloam, while terebinths, acacias, and occasional palm-trees, inclining their pale crests, towered over them. There, sweet marjorams grew, grey irises, thyme, verbena, and the red roses of Sharon. Below these clumps of star-studded bushes, age-old reefs stretched out, while springs of pure water, the fountain's tributaries, babbled in their tracks.*" (Gérard de Nerval, Journey to the Orient, 1844 [trans. P. Owen, 1972], p. 238)

A mug-like vessel made of chalk that could not become impure and was very fashionable in the 1st century C.E.

Top: the traditional Tomb of Absalom situated in the Kidron Valley in Jerusalem. *Bottom*: the traditional Tomb of Zechariah and (*left*) a stone ossuary (bone-box) found within a tomb in Jerusalem bearing the incised Aramaic inscription of Simon the temple-builder.

Bottom: a general view of the Field of Blood, known as Akeldama, and the Greek Orthodox Monastery of Saint Onyphrius. *Left*: glass vessels from a tomb excavated in Akeldama, and (*right*) an ossuary with a carving of the façade of the Jewish Temple between two rosettes.

Tombs: Kidron Valley and Akeldama

Surrounding Jerusalem is a vast necropolis of more than one thousand rock-hewn tombs dating from Early Roman times. Most of them consist of small rectangular chambers with tunnel-like burial recesses and benches in their walls. The dead were laid to rest on benches and when their bodies had decomposed, the bones were gathered within stone boxes (ossuaries) usually ornamented with rosettes (symbolic cherubim) and other geometric designs. Occasionally inscriptions were scrawled on the sides of the ossuaries. One ossuary bore the inscription: "Simon, builder of the temple", perhaps indicating that he was one of the workers employed in building the Jewish Temple in Jerusalem. In a tomb excavated north of the city at Givat Hamivtar, the remains of a crucified man have also been found. The description of the tomb of Jesus in the Gospels suggests that it was a small tomb of the type well known around Jerusalem and since it was a "new" tomb recesses may still not have been carved into the walls like other family tombs of that period.

Some of the most impressive tomb monuments are situated in the Kidron Valley, virtually opposite the east wall of the Temple Mount, namely the pyramid-roofed Tomb of Zachariah and the hat-shaped Tomb of Absalom. The latter has been identified with Absalom since medieval times, in reference to 2 Samuel 18:18 where it is stated that Absalom set up for himself a "pillar" in the King's Valley. In Arabic it is known as "Tantour Firaoun" (Pharoah's crown). The monument is free-standing and the lower part is rock-cut whereas the upper hat-like part was built of well-dressed stones. Access to the inner tomb chamber of the Tomb of Absalom is usually not possible because the entrance is more than ten meters up the side of a vertical south wall and one would have to have all the appropriate climbing gear to get up there. One day in the summer of 2000 I received a telephone call from Joe Zias: "scaffolding is going up tomorrow morning on the south side of the Tomb of Absalom – would you like to come and have a look?" I answered in the affirmative. This was a rare and exciting chance at seeing the monument up close. It was worth it. The inner chamber is almost square and three steps lead into it.

The chamber originally had two benches with shallow headrests within arched recesses and a ceiling ornamented with a sunken panel with a central wreath and four small circles in relief. Another interesting cemetery is that of Akeldama, situated at the junction of the Kidron and Hinnom Valleys to the south of Mount Zion. This is where, according to Gospel tradition, the potter's field was bought using the 30 pieces of silver which Judas cast down in the Temple (Matthew 27: 3-8; Acts 1:19). Numerous rock-cut tombs have been investigated in this area since the early explorations of the nineteenth century, notably in recent years with the excavation of a multi-chambered tomb with unique finds close to the road below, and with the discovery of another tomb containing a shroud dating from the first-century C.E., the first ever found in Jerusalem.

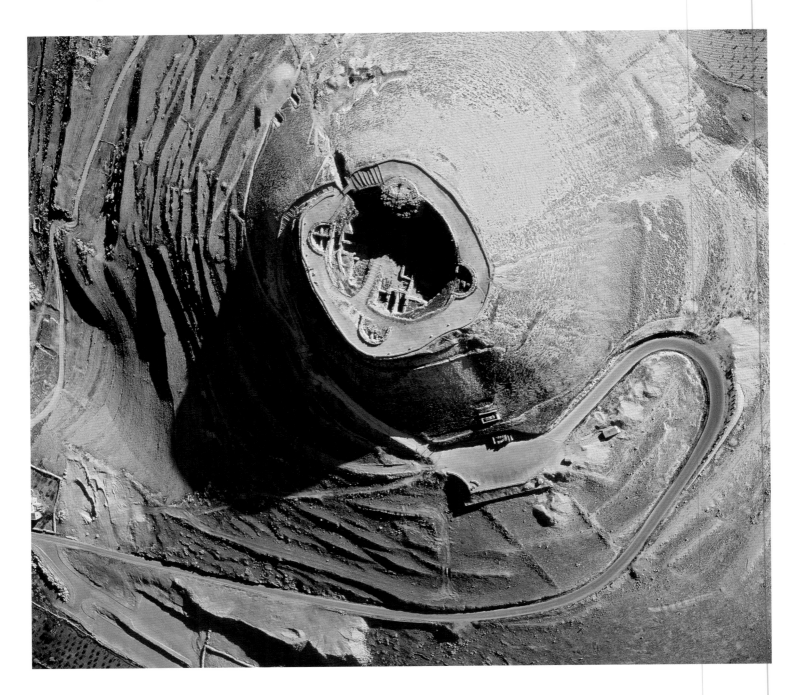

Herodium

The palace-fortress of Herodium (Jebel Fureidis), situated southeast of Jerusalem, is an interesting site for three reasons: first, in terms of landscaping it is unique in the architectural history of the land; second, it was built to commemorate a decisive battle which took place between Herod the Great and the Hasmoneans in 40 B.C.E. (had the battle gone differently the history of the region would have been quite different), and finally it is the site of Herod's mausoleum.

Although extensive excavations have been undertaken at the site, it was only recently (in March 2007) that the exact burial place of Herod the Great was discovered on the north-east slope of the prominent palace-fortress. The substantial foundations of a platform for a funerary monument were unearthed, made of finely-dressed rectangular stones (ashlars); it was situated next to the "steep ascent" of steps mentioned by the ancient historian Josephus Flavius. In the surrounding fills archaeologists uncovered tens of fragments of a very large stone sarcophagus, decorated with rosette carvings, which may have held the body of Herod himself. Archaeologists who have been studying the mystery of the hidden tomb of Herod the Great are very satisfied with the results. However, there are still two mysteries to solve: where are his mortal remains? And who were the people who smashed his sarcophagus to smithereens? Herod surely, somewhere, is having the last laugh.

Ashlar platform for Herod's funerary monument.

Top Left and right: vertical and oblique views of the fortress of Herodium.

Top: the fortress after a fall of snow. *Bottom*: the inner columned courtyard of the fortress (*left*), and a decorated mosaic floor (*right*).

"…Herod constructed another fortress in the region where he had defeated the Jews after his expulsion from the realm, when Antigonus was in power. This fortress, which is some sixty stades distant from Jerusalem, is naturally strong and very suitable for such a structure, for reasonably nearby is a hill, raised to a [greater] height by the hand of man and rounded off in the shape of a breast. At intervals it has round towers, and it has a steep ascent formed of two hundred steps of hewn stone. Within it are costly apartments made for security and for ornament at the same time. At the base of the hill there are pleasure grounds built in such a way as to be worth seeing, among other things because of the way in which water, which is lacking in that place, is brought in from a distance and at great expense. The surrounding plain was built up as a city second to none, with the hill serving as an acropolis for the other dwellings." (Josephus, Jewish Antiquities, XV, 323-325).

Solomon's Pools

Two of the three pools situated close to Bethlehem and named after Solomon, were built to regulate and store water derived from local springs, and water was conveyed from there by aqueduct to Jerusalem in Roman times. According to legend this was the place where Solomon came to relax and collect his thoughts among the leafy gardens and bubbling waters. Today, unfortunately, judging by my most recent visit to the site in 2006, the pools are mostly dry and the immediate area is being used for rubbish disposal.

A closer view of one of the pools empty of water during a dry spell.
Top: a general view of the pools, with the Ottoman fort on the lower left of the picture, and with the Judean Desert in the background.

Hebron and the Tombs of the Hebrew Patriarchs

Within the heart of Hebron, hemmed in on almost all sides by buildings and houses, is a site sacred to Jews, Christians and Moslems alike, since it is where traditionally the Patriarchs Abraham, Isaac and Jacob are said to have been buried. According to the Bible, Abraham, wishing to provide a suitable

burial place for Sarah, acquired a field with a double cave from Ephron the Hittite for 400 silver shekels (Genesis 23: 19). Known in Hebrew as the Cave of Machpelah and in Arabic as the Haram el-Khalil, the enclosure that one sees today was originally constructed at the time of Herod the Great, and the stonework of the indented exterior walls of the enclosure are quite remarkable and are distinguished by drafted-margin masonry, with some blocks up to 7.5 meters in length. These walls provide an idea of how the enclosure walls of Herod's Temple in Jerusalem may have appeared.

Two views of the Haram el-Khalil compound within the modern city of Hebron (*right* and *bottom*). *Left*: the tombs of the Hebrew Patriarchs within the enclosure.

"And after this, Abraham buried Sarah his wife in the cave of the field of Machpelah before Mamre: the same is Hebron in the land of Canaan. And the field and the cave that is therein, were made sure unto Abraham for a possession of a burying place by the sons of Heth." (Genesis 23: 19-20).

Top: a general view of the ruins of Qumran which was the home to the Dead Sea Scrolls sect. Visible in the background is the Dead Sea. *Opposite*: a leather sandal.

Qumran and the Dead Sea Scrolls

Qumran is known worldwide as the place where the famous Dead Sea Scrolls were found. In 1947 a boy from the Ta'amireh Bedouin tribe crawled into the darkness of a cave and made an astounding discovery that changed scholarship of the Second Temple period topsy-turvy virtually overnight. What the lad discovered were two-thousand year old scrolls. The scrolls include a variety of religious and sectarian documents, all of which apparently originated in the library of a community of people who called themselves *yahad* (literally "togetherness"). The general consensus of opinion is that they

must be the same as the sect of the Essenes mentioned briefly by Pliny the Elder and in the writings of Josephus Flavius. Eventually these scrolls and others fragments were turned over to the antiquities market and thus indirectly came to the attention of scholars. Once it became clear that the scrolls had come from caves close to Qumran, archaeologists moved in and began digging in the caves and at the ancient settlement. The settlement itself is not spectacular in appearance: simple stone walls, various buildings, channels and water installations. Archaeologists, however, never find Qumran boring and they will always be returning to investigate the mysteries of the site and the caves in their surrounding landscape.

The Essenes as described by Josephus Flavius: *"Before the sun is up they utter no word on mundane matters, but offer to Him certain prayers, which have been handed down from their forefathers, as though entreating him to rise. They are then dismissed by their superiors to the various crafts in which they are severally proficient and are strenuously employed until the fifth hour, when they again assemble in one place, and, after girding their loins with linen cloths, bathe their bodies in cold water. After this purification, they assemble in a private apartment which none have of the uninitiated is permitted to enter; pure now themselves, they repair to the refectory, as to some sacred shrine. When they have taken their seats in silence, the baker serves out the loaves to them in order, and the cook sets before each one plate with a single course. Before meat, the priest says a grace; thus at the beginning and the close they do homage to God as the bountiful giver of life. Then laying aside their rainment, as holy vestments, they do betake themselves to their labors until evening. On their return they sup in like manner."* (Jewish Wars II, viii, 5).

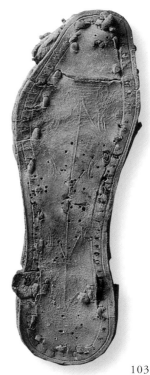

The openings to caves where some of the Dead Sea Scrolls were found.

Two fragments of scrolls.

"Knowing that there might still be a scroll or two, or a heap of torn fragments, buried somewhere within a crevice at the back of one of the caves, is the sort of thing that gives the scholar a kind of buzz that ordinarily can only be obtained through smoking illegal substances. Qumran, it has to be said, is a bit like the proverbial honey pot, and it has managed to bring out the worst and the best in international scholarship" (S. Gibson, The Cave of John the Baptist, 2004, p. 146).

Harbors along the Dead Sea

Although Khirbet Qumran may very well have been the settlement of the sect of the Essenes, many archaeologists believe it was not just a place of prayer and meditation but that it also had a thriving economy. In summer it can be hellishly hot with temperatures reaching some 40 degrees Celsius. Surrounding the settlement were groves of palm trees and perhaps even small gardens. Members of the Qumran community probably participated in various trading ventures relating to the transportation of balsam oils and commodities such as salt and bitumen from the Dead Sea. Various harbor installations have been found along the shores of the Dead Sea, notably those at Khirbet Mazin and Rujm el-Bahr.

Khirbet Mazin, fortress and wharf remains.

105

The site of the Hasmonean and Herodian palaces at Tulul Abu-Alayiq, looking towards the north.

Jericho: Herodian Winter Palaces

One of the swimming pools attached to the palace at Jericho was the scene of the murder of an exceptionally handsome 17-year old youth named Aristobulus. The murder marked a turning point in the clash between King Herod and the Hasmonean family. Aristobulus, against Herod's wishes and notwithstanding his age, was openly proclaimed as high priest in Jerusalem. This gave Herod an enormous dose of anxiety. While a guest at the Hasmonean winter palace at Jericho, with Alexandra, mother of Aristobulus, as hostess, Herod executed a devious plan to eliminate Aristobulus and to try to make it look like an accident.

Excavations at Tulul Abu-Alayiq close to modern Jericho, have brought to light the remains of the Hasmonean palace with two attached swimming pools. Herod the Great subsequently went on to build a series of magnificent palaces at the spot and these too have been uncovered by archaeologists, showing that they included pavilions, reception halls, baths and even gardens. Roman dignitaries could have been entertained there and they would have felt perfectly at home. By all accounts Herod was a prolific and imaginative builder, even though like many contemporary monarchs, he possessed an unforgiving and murderous streak in his character. In 4 B.C.E. Herod died of failure of the heart and kidneys following a malingering illness, accompanied by bouts of uncontrollable anger and cruelty.

"When the festival was over and they were being entertained at Jericho as the guests of Alexandra, he [Herod] showed great friendliness to the youth [Aristobulus] and led him on to drink without fear, and he was ready to join in his play and to act like a young man in order to please him. But as the place was naturally hot, they soon went out in a group for a stroll, and stood beside the swimming pools, of which there were several large ones around the palace, and cooled themselves off from the excessive heat of noon. At first they watched some of the servants and friends [of Herod] as they swam, and then, at Herod's urging, the youth was induced [to join them].
But with the darkness coming on while he swam, some of the friends, who had been given the orders to do so, kept pressing him down and holding him under water as if in sport, and they did not let him up until they had quite suffocated him." (Josephus, Jewish Antiquities, XV, 53-56).

Top: collapsed brick columns in the area of the sunken gardens.
Bottom: a general view of the excavations while they were in progress. Note the prominent swimming pool in centre, right of the picture.

"I returned behind Alexandra's palace and walked in the wadi, which had pools of water standing everywhere. These were connected by the tiniest of brooks, smaller than the flow of a half-opened faucet, which murmured softly in the perfect silence, and sometimes a loose stone would fall in the shadows behind me, or some night bird would suddenly rush overhead. What a feeling of solitude!" (Egon H. E. Lass, The Seasons of Tulul, 2005, p. 91)

The fortress of Masada lit up at night. *Opposite:* north end of Masada showing the terraced palace. On top of the hill are long storerooms and a bath-house.

Masada

Masada is truly a magnificent archaeological site. A lofty fortress situated on the eastern edge of the Judean Desert overlooking the Dead Sea, it witnessed one of the dramatic episodes in the history of the Jewish people and was the stage for the final act of resistance against the Romans. The best source regarding Masada and its fall are the writings of the first-century historian Josephus Flavius (*Jewish Wars* 2: 477; 7: 252-253). Excavated in the 1960s by the famous general/politician/archaeologist, Yigael Yadin, the discoveries included luxurious palaces, one marvelously hanging on to the northern cliff-edge of the mountain and constructed on different levels, a large bath-house, storerooms, casemate walls, a ritual bathing pool (*mikve*), large reservoirs and a synagogue. A number of ancient manuscripts were found, notably a copy of Ecclesiasticus, and various potsherds bearing names in ink (*ostraca*). Built by Herod the Great, the fortress was defended for three years by the Zealots after the fall of Jerusalem in 70 C.E. It finally fell to the Roman governor, Flavius Silva, when he laid siege to the fortress, building an enormous ramp of earth and large stones against its western flank. Once the Romans managed to breach the fortress wall, the defenders, under the leadership of Eleazar Ben Yair, decided "neither to serve the Romans nor any other save God" and committed suicide.

Potsherds found in the excavations inscribed with Hebrew names.

Yadin identified eleven of the Masada ostraca, one of which mentions Ben-Yair, with the "lots" used by the defenders in carrying out their mass suicide: "Had we indeed found the very ostraca which had been used in the casting of the lots? We shall never know for certain. But the probability is strengthened by the fact that among these eleven inscribed pieces of pottery was one bearing the name 'Ben Ya'ir'. The inscription of plain 'Ben Ya'ir' on Masada at that particular time could have referred to none other than Eleazar Ben Yair."

(Y. Yadin, Masada, 1966, p. 197).

One of the Roman military camps with Masada in the distance.

"They then chose ten men by lot out of them, to slay all the rest; everyone of whom laid himself down by his wife and children on the ground, and threw his arms about them and they offered their necks to the stroke of those who by lot executed that melancholy office; and when these ten had, without fear, slain them all, they made the same rule for casting lots for themselves, that he whose lot it was to first kill the other nine, and after all, should kill himself." (Josephus, Jewish War 7:395)

The Roman camp situated above the Cave of Letters in Nahal Hever.

Judean Desert Caves and Bar Kokhba's Rebellion

There was absolute silence in the hall. It was electrifying. It was the occasion of a lecture given by Yigael Yadin at the President's House in Jerusalem in 1960. Yadin flashed a slide onto a screen showing an ancient document he had just uncovered in one of the Judean Desert Caves, and read aloud the first line of writing on it: "Shimeon bar Kosiba, President over Israel". He then turned to the then President of Israel Ben-Zvi and addressed him by saying: "Your Excellency, I am honored to be able to tell you that we have discovered fifteen dispatches written or dictated by the last President of Israel 1800 years ago." The silence in the hall was suddenly broken by spontaneous cries of joy and excitement. During 1960-1961 a methodical cave-by-cave search was made of the sheer walls of the wadis that drop down to the Dead Sea, led by archaeologists and facilitated by volunteers and soldiers. Finds were made from the Chalcolithic and Iron Age periods, but the most important finds were of scrolls and documents and objects that were hidden away by Jewish refugees at the time of the Second Revolt against the Romans (132-135 C.E.). In Nahal Hever a Roman siege camp was found on the edge of the precipice which was built to prevent the refugees hidden in the caves below from escaping. In one of these caves – nicknamed the "Cave of Horrors" – archaeologists encountered a gruesome sight: some 40 skeletons of adults, children and even babies.

"I did not dare touch the papyri themselves, but I managed carefully to pull out of the bundle two of the four wooden slats which I had observed in the cave. The other two were still folded inside the bundle. The two I took out had clear letters in ink, in cursive writing of the type discovered at Murabba'at. I copied the letters on to a piece of paper, one by one. My hand copied automatically without my mind registering the words. When I finally looked at what I had scribbled, I could not believe my eyes. It read: 'Shimeon bar Kosiba, President over Israel'! I rushed to my wife Carmella and told her. 'Are you sure or is this another hallucination?', she said…" (Yigael Yadin, Bar Kokhba, 1971, p. 122).

A manuscript letter written by Shimon Bar Kokhba, found in Wadi Muraba'at (*top*), and (*bottom*) the Cave of Letters in Nahal Hever.

Letter from Bar Kokhba found in Wadi Murabba'at: "From Shimeon [ben/bar Kosiba], peace! Send cereals five kors of wheat to ……. I have ordered someone to give you his wheat after Sabbath they will take."

Nabateans in the Negev Desert

Moa

Petra

The Nabateans are a fascinating people with obscure origins. They may originally have come from as far as Qedar or the Persian Gulf, or, alternatively, they may have come from the Arabian Hejaz. One thing is certain by 312 B.C.E. they had already established their center at Petra and were able to successfully defend themselves from an attack by Antigonus the "one-eyed", a veteran of the eastern campaigns of Alexander the Great.

The Nabateans were the ultimate tradesmen. Petra (referred to as *Raqmu* by the Nabateans) was the center for the redistribution of caravan goods from the east; an important trading route led from the direction of the city through the

Negev Desert to the west. There are at least six major Nabatean settlements in the Negev, namely Nessana, Shivta, Haluza, Avdat, Rehovot-in-the-Negev, and Mampsis. The Nabateans were extremely proficient at water conservation in desert conditions, building extremely advanced hydraulic engineering systems, but they did not build the extensive agricultural terraces in the Negev desert as many scholars have hitherto assumed; they were apparently built later in the Byzantine and Umayyad periods instead. The Nabateans spoke Arabic but their *lingua franca* was Aramaic. Their main deities were Dushara (male) and Al 'Uzza (female). They had a distinctive painted pottery which made its appearance around 100 B.C.E. The earliest coins were struck between 62-60 B.C.E.

An oil press uncovered at Moa.

Pliny the Elder described the trade route in the first century C.E.:
"Frankincense cannot be exported [from Arabia] except through the land
of the Gebanites, and so a tax is paid to their king too. From Thomna,
their capital, to Gaza is … sixty-five camel stages… All along the road
there are expenses, here for water, there for food or lodging at the halts
and various tolls, so that the expenditure for each camel is 688 denarii
as far as the Mediterranean, and then another tax is paid to the
publicans of the Roman empire." (quoted in Nelson Glueck, *Rivers in the Desert:*
A History of the Negev, 1968, p. 270).

Top: a general view of the buildings uncovered at Moa. *Bottom*: two lamps, a jug and a typical painted Nabatean bowl.

Top: the Roman theatre at Sepphoris. *Bottom*: the excavations of Sepphoris in progress.

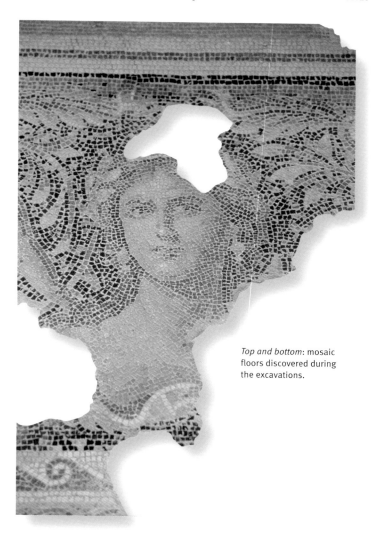

Top and bottom: mosaic floors discovered during the excavations.

Sepphoris (Diocaesarea)

It was in a strong snowstorm that Herod the Great finally managed to conquer the small town of Sepphoris in the Lower Galilee and to make it his own, but on his death the locals, led by Judas son of Ezekias, exacted their revenge by pillaging his royal palace. Revenge is a strong emotion. Subsequently, under his son Herod Antipas, Sepphoris grew and expanded, blossoming into a major city, the capital of Galilee. Following the Jewish Revolt against the Romans, after Vespasian conferred the status of *polis* on the city, Hadrian renamed it Diocaesarea and the city was in due course graced with many fine buildings, notably the Capitoline temple and a theater, and large dwellings with very fine decorated floors. In the late second and early third centuries C.E. Sepphoris became the seat of the Jewish Sanhedrin under Rabbi Judah Ha-Nasi, and it is said that he might have edited the Mishna there.

Yodefat (Jotapata)

Situated not far from Sepphoris, Yodefat was fortified by Josephus (who at that time was a Jewish fighter but later became renowned as an historian) but in 67 C.E. Vespasian and his Roman soldiers laid siege to the place; after 47 days it was forced to capitulate.

Yodefat was a small Jewish town with houses and simple ritual bathing pools (*mikva'ot*). Some of the houses were quite palatial and recent archaeological excavations have brought to light rooms covered with colorful wall paintings and stucco reliefs. Stark remains of the battle resulting from Vespasian's siege of the town include ballista balls and iron bow and catapult arrowheads. The Jewish defenders hurriedly tried to add defenses to the site before the arrival of the Romans, but to no avail.

Gamla

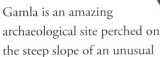

Gamla is an amazing archaeological site perched on the steep slope of an unusual hill shaped like the hump of a camel in the Golan Heights. Since the nineteenth century scholars argued about the location of Gamla which was destroyed by the Romans in 67 C.E. and described in the writings of the historian Josephus Flavius. It was only in 1968 that the exact location of the site was finally confirmed. Archaeological excavations conducted at the site since 1976 have brought to light a fascinating array of remains of the first-century town, including fortifications, houses, an oil press and a large public assembly building which has been identified as a synagogue. Arrowheads and stone ballista balls, and burning and scorching marks attest to the Roman siege of the town.

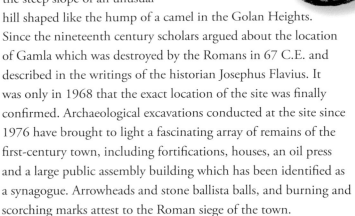

Top: a general view of the site of Yodefat. *Bottom*: Two views of the synagogue uncovered at Gamla, and (*above*) coins derived from the excavations.

A view of the camel-hump appearance of Gamla, with the Byzantine and Ottoman village in the foreground.

"*Then the Romans brought up the rams at three points, and battering their way through the wall poured in through the breaches with a great blare of trumpets and din of weapons, and shouting themselves hoarse flung themselves upon the defenders of the town.*"

(Josephus, Jewish Wars, 4.1-83)

A Herodian agricultural estate at Horvat Aqav above the Sharon Plain. The smaller rectangular area represents the rebuilding of the estate on a smaller scale in the Byzantine period.

Ramat Ha-Nadiv

Situated on top of the southern Carmel Hill range, within the grounds of the Ramat Ha-Nadiv park where the Baron de Rothschild is buried, are two interesting ancient sites, namely Horvat Eleq and Horvat Aqav. The first is located next to a spring and has the remains of a fortified palatial structure – probably a large rural estate – dating back to Second Temple times, as well as a bath-house with mosaic floors. An exciting find was made next to the entrance to the spring: a total of 2000 coins dating from the 4th to 6th centuries C.E. The second site has two superimposed farmsteads, the lower from the Herodian period and the upper from the Byzantine period. From the latter site there is a breathtaking view of the Sharon Plain and behind it the Mediterranean Sea.

Fortified Herodian remains and a spring at Horvat Eleq (*left*), and (*right*) a wine jar from the excavations.

Shuni Mayumas

Ramat Ha-Nadiv
Shuni

Not far from Ramat Ha-Nadiv is the site of Shuni, which has a spring of water which many believed had miraculous powers. The Bordeaux Pilgrim, for example, in 332 C.E. reported on the belief that should a woman enter the water she would immediately fall pregnant. The story of the strange goings-on at Shuni may be traced back to Roman times when pagan water festivals were performed at the site, with rampant sexual orgies and overflowing jugs of wine playing their part. Archaeological excavations have uncovered a very large and mysterious semi-circular pool behind the theatre with a mosaic floor with built-in recesses for flags and marked with lines and lanes, presumably denoting the directions of the water games and the positions taken by the players. According to Melalus from Antioch such festivals were performed in honor of Dionysus and Aphrodite every three years, they tended to last 30 days, and some of the stage performances were celebrated at night. It must have been a colorful scene, but definitely not the sort of place you would want to take your children.

A mosaic floor with a Greek inscription, and (*right*) Roman statuary found in the Shuni excavations. *Bottom*: a general view of the Shuni site with an octagonal church in the foreground, and the Roman theater behind.

Caesarea Maritima

Founded in honor of Caesar Augustus by Herod the Great, the city and its harbor developed and grew rapidly, with the grandeur of the city in the first-century well reflected in the writings of Josephus Flavius. Caesarea was also the scene of the trial and eventual imprisonment of St. Paul, and it was from there that he was taken in chains to Rome. Two of its famous inhabitants included Origen and Eusebius, who taught in the Christian school, which had an astounding library.

Hence, it is not surprising that out of this city came the famous translation of the Bible known as the Hexapla.

Archaeological excavations have uncovered many parts of the city adjacent to the seashore and in the area of the harbor, notably a theater, which has been conserved and is used for modern stage performances, a race-course extending parallel to the shoreline, a praetorium and palace complex, the city wall, a hippodrome with an Aswan-granite obelisk, a bath-house, and numerous churches.

Top: the theatre at Caesarea. *Bottom*: the harbor.

"[the soldiers] when they came to Caesarea, and delivered the epistle to the governor, presented Paul also before him. And when the governor had read the letter, he asked of what province he [Paul] was. And when he understood that he was of Cilicia. I will hear thee, said he, when thine accusers are also come. And he commanded him to be kept in Herod's judgement hall." (Acts 23: 33-35).

The race course with part of the praetorium in the foreground.

The aqueduct built on arches which brought water to Caesarea.

A Latin inscription mentioning Pontius Pilate and the emperor Tiberius was discovered at Caesarea in 1961 and indicates that the title of the governor of Judea was also praefectus. *It reads "...this Tiberium, Pontius Pilate, prefect of Judea, did [or erected]...", but the rest of the inscription is not extant. Pilate is best known in regard to the trial and crucifixion of Jesus.*

The hippodrome with an obelisk (*left*) and the fragmentary inscription mentioning Pontius Pilate (*right*).

A vertical view of the harbor of Caesarea, with the ancient Roman harbor represented as black shadows underwater.

Top and right: two views of the excavations in progress.

Ashkelon

As one of the major cities on the Mediterranean Coast, Ashkelon was endowed by Herod the Great with "baths, magnificent fountains, and colonnaded quadrangles, remarkable for both scale and craftsmanship" (Josephus, *Jewish Wars* 1:422). The first substantial remains of the Hellenistic and Roman cities of Ashkelon were brought to light by British archaeologists working at the site in the early 1920s. This included a building of the Roman period that has been identified as a council-house (*bouleuterion*). It had a theater-shaped structure at one end and was entered through a colonnaded forecourt with columns surmounted by Corinthian capitals. On the external wall of the chamber were sculpted winged victories, one standing on a globe borne by Atlas, holding wreaths and palm branches. Local pagan cults flourished in Roman *Ascalon*, but the make-up of the city was entirely cosmopolitan and there was a large Jewish community in the city as well. Quite a few fragments of Roman sculptures have been recovered from the site, including those of deities and a massive foot of a giant sculpture, as well as an impressive sarcophagus depicting the battle with the Amazons, which is now in the courtyard of the Rockefeller Museum in Jerusalem. Recent excavations have brought to light a Byzantine-period building – perhaps a brothel – with an inscription on the outside of a plastered bath reading "Enter and Rejoice".

Various pieces of Roman statuary from the site, including a sarcophagus depicting the battle with the Amazons, female and male figures, and a giant marble floor.

*Strabo of Amaseia (first century C.E.): "The country of
the Ascalonitae excels in onion, but the town is small.
Antiochus the philosopher, who was born a little
before my time, was a native of this place."*

(M. Stern, Greek and Latin Authors on Jews and Judaism,
1974, Vol. I, p. 291)

Top: a mosaic floor fragment with a Greek inscription.

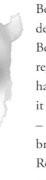

Beth Guvrin

Beth Guvrin owes its rise to power to the demise of its sister-city neighboring Maresha. Beth Guvrin replaced the other as an important regional city when Maresha was destroyed by the hands of the Parthians in 40 B.C.E. In 200 C.E. it was renamed Eleutheropolis – "city of the free" – by Septimus Severus. Recent excavations have brought to light a remarkable well-preserved Roman amphitheatre and a bath-house, as well as later remains, including a Crusader Church.

Large hewn bell-shaped caverns existing in the area of Beth Guvrin, created owing to the local ancient practice of quarrying for soft chalk, are extremely beautiful and photogenic, often serving as venues for classical music concerts.

A general view of the excavated part of Beth Guvrin, showing the amphitheater in the center.

The ancient columned street, now a pastoral scene.

Sebastia

Although Micah gave a prophecy that God "will make Samaria as a heap in the field" (Micah 1:6), there is actually a modern village, known as Sabastiyeh, to the east of the ancient tell. There can be no doubt that by the Roman period Samaria was at its peak, and when Herod the Great was given the city by Augustus, he had it embellished, renaming it Sebastia in honor of his benefactor (Greek *sebastos* = Augustus). The city was well fortified with city gates and strong walls. A colonnaded street led through the city. On the acropolis was a temple dedicated to Augustus, a temple dedicated to the goddess Kore (with a sculpted relief found there depicting a *Dioscuri* cap topped by a star), a forum and other buildings. Numerous sculptures were found. Excavations have shown that even the domestic dwellings were palatial in character, and numerous fragments of decorated wall plaster were uncovered.

A statue of the goddess Kore (*left*), and (*right*) a view of the forum. *Center*: a fragment of a wall painting, a relief with a Dioscuri cap, and a bust of a dignitary.

One of the city gates of Samaria with the countryside beyond. *Bottom*: a temple (*left*) and theatre (*right*).

At the watering-hole (Jacob's well), Jesus encountered a woman who had come to draw water and asks for water: "How is it that thou [she asks Jesus] being a Jew, asketh drink from me, which am a woman of Samaria? For the Jews have no dealings with Samaritans." (John 4:9).

Nablus

The Roman city of Flavia Neapolis is situated beneath the modern city of Nablus and remains of it can only be seen here and there, when the ground is opened up in archaeological excavations. In fact, archaeologists have managed to uncover a wide colonnaded street, a hippodrome, segments of the city wall and large baths. An inscription indicates that wrestling games were performed within the city. A magnificent decorated mosaic floor from a Roman mansion was also uncovered.

Top, *center and right*: three views of Nablus with Tell Balata in the foreground. *Bottom*: the border of a Roman mosaic depicting a mask and a hunter.

Mazor

A curious, solitary building in the middle of the landscape, on the road between Lod and Migdal Aphek, turns out to be a Roman mausoleum. It was first investigated by the British Consul in Palestine James Finn in the 1850s, and later in more recent times by archaeologists. It seems to have been snatched from the teeth of destructing owing to it having been transformed into a Moslem shrine dedicated to Neby Yahya. Dated to around 300 C.E. the mausoleum consists of a columned porch leading into a double burial chamber in which sarcophagi were situated. Small niches in the interior walls were presumably used for the cremated remains of family members of retainers. Remains of a large Hellenistic settlement have recently been uncovered nearby.

The mausoleum at Mazor.

Architectural fragment from Banias.

Banias

With the snow-topped Hermon range looming above and with the source of the Jordan River bubbling out of the mountain, Banias is an impressive site, attracting people to it from very early times. It is not surprising, therefore, that monumental buildings have been uncovered by archaeologists at the site, notably a cultic compound from the Roman period with at least two temples, dedicated to Zeus and Pan, with numerous discoveries of statuary, and a large palace in the lower part of the city, with halls and courts and underground corridors, which was built in the first century C.E.

The temple compound and the source of the Jordan River.

The site of the large monumental palace (*left*). and (*above*) a reconstruction of the original appearance of the temple compound.

"...and through Druse territory he [Burckhardt] came eventually to Banias, the ancient Caesarea Phillipi and the Dan of the Jews – a place originally devoted to the worship of Pan. Here he was able to make a sketch. As it was then Ramadan, the Fasting Month, he often sat up late at night under the trees, smoking and talking with his guide and any local villagers who came to join them. When he ran out of money he began to return, going south of Mount Hermon across Jebel Heish; beyond lay those ports of the desert, Damascus, Homs and Hama, and the great desert itself unfolding ever eastward in jewel blue veils of shimmering light." (K. Sim, Jean Louis Burckhardt: A Biography, 1981, pp. 91-92)

Right: a rock-hewn cultic niche in the area of the temple compound.

Signet ring
encased in gold.

Sussita Hippos

A German engineer named
Gottlieb Schumacher undertook
a remarkable survey of the
antiquities of the Golan Heights.
Upon reaching a site called
Kulat el-Husn in June 1885,
he found substantial ruins
there, suggesting that it should
be identified with Hippos
mentioned by Josephus Flavius.
Overlooking the Sea of Galilee from the east,
Hippos-Sussita has breathtaking views in all
directions. Recent archaeological excavations at
the site have brought to light a large paved area
of Roman date, perhaps a forum, as well as a
street, a large water reservoir, and later Byzantine
churches. A hoard of gold jewelry was found
within the *diakonikon* of the north-east church.

Fallen columns, perhaps the result of an earthquake.

An excavated church (*left*), and (*right*) a hoard of metal vessels.

A general view of Hippos-Sussita.

A basalt carving (*left*)
and a segment of a
mosaic floor with a
Greek inscription.

"The examination of the ruins could only be done disjointedly, according as the object of the work above pointed out. I cannot, therefore, unconditionally guarantee an uninterrupted completeness in the description of the ruined places with which the Jaulan [Golan] is swarming, for in addition to this the great distrust exhibited by the natives against travelers increases the difficulties of the examination of the land. The natives from fear of new taxes took care to conceal almost everything, so that information and guides could only be reached by threats of prison, and, as a rule, the discovering of ruins had to depend entirely upon myself." (G. Schumacher, The Jaulan, 1888, p. 6)

A general view of the
excavations with the
Sea of Galilee behind.

Kedesh

In the nineteenth century explorers of the Palestine Exploration Fund arrived and expressed awe at the preservation of a Roman temple at the site of Qades (Kedesh). There was also a monumental mausoleum at the site, to the west, which the explorers photographed not long before the local inhabitants began dismantling its walls, popping individual blocks one-by-one into a kiln in order to make quicklime. The temple, however, survived on the flanks of the ancient mound of Kedesh and was re-surveyed and partly excavated by Tel Aviv University in the early 1980s. It dates from the second and third centuries C.E. and according to an inscription was dedicated to the "Holy God of the Sky", to the Syro-Phoenician god Baal Shamin. Thousands of *bullae* (stamped seals from documents) were discovered in recent excavations of the Hellenistic settlement on the mound.

The façade of the temple at Kedesh. *Bottom*: a general view of the site (*left*) and an upturned Corinthian capital (*right*).

Letter of Captain Charles Wilson to the Palestine Exploration Fund of 20 January 1866: "At Kedes some excavations were made on the site of the ruins: the western building is a tomb containing eleven loculi, the eastern is a temple of the sun of about the same date as Baalbek. The lintel over the main entrance was dug up; on its underside is a large figure of the sun (I think), and over the architrave is a small cornice beautifully worked; it consists of a scroll of vine leaves, with bunches of grapes; in the centre is a bust, and facing it on either side is the figure of a stag. On either side of the main entrance is a small niche with a hole communicating to larger niches within the building, like a sort of confessional..." (PEF Proceedings and Notes, 1865-69, p.30)

139

Ancient inscription from Hamath Gader: "The tholos of the lukewarm pool should be named after another Caesarean, Leo, as it once [used to be named] after Alexander". (trans. L. Di Segni)

A general view of the Hamath Gader baths with the Yarmuk River visible behind. *Bottom*: one of the many Greek inscriptions found in the baths.

Hamath Gader

Situated on the right bank of the River Yarmuk is a town with remains from the Roman and Byzantine periods, and a number of springs of water in the plain, in which some, especially the hot springs (hence Hamath Gader, Hebrew for the "hot springs of Gader"), were ascribed medicinal properties, and for that reason people flocked to the site from all directions to lower their ill and fatigued bodies into the sumptuous bath complex located there.

Dover

Further up the River Yarmuk is another site, Tel Dover, which was excavated by archaeologists in the 1990s in an emergency operation owing to the planned construction of a dam – a joint Israeli/Jordanian initiative – which was never built. Remains of housing units, alleyways and courtyards were found from Roman, Byzantine and Early Islamic periods.

A general view of the Dover excavations. *Bottom:* one of the bath chambers at Hamath Gader.

Ancient inscription from Hamath Gader: "Be no longer in dread of the water-carrying bath being smashed, which brought infinite sorrows to many, by hurting and killing men, in many cases children, for the [yawning] earth buried it all from above. But now, having laid a pavement [on either side], made a sporting place Nikas [?], having let pleasant water to be drawn elsewhere." (trans. L Di Segni)

141

Beth Shean

According to the Roman writer Pliny a league of ten cities – the Decapolis – once existed east of the Jordan. It also including the city of Beth Shean (known then as Scythopolis) which was located in the northern Jordan Valley at the junction of a number of important highways. Major excavations have been conducted within the area of the Roman and Byzantine civic center of Beth Shean, in the shadow of the imposing biblical mound. The city was once very impressive judging by the colonnaded streets, baths, temples, a nymphaeum, theater and amphitheater, uncovered by archaeologists in recent decades. A number of Byzantine churches have also been unearthed, including the remains of the Monastery of Lady Mary (Kyria Maria) to the northwest of the city, with exquisite mosaic floors.

Top: a general view of the Roman and Byzantine city of Beth Shean. *Bottom*: a segment of a decorated mosaic floor in the Monastery of St. Mary.

A view of the city fortifications with the ancient mound in the background (*left*), and (*right*) the amphitheatre.

The columned street of Roman and Byzantine Beth Shean, with the ancient mound in the background.

Shalem (Salim)

In July 1975 an American stockbroker made the chance discovery of a lifetime at Tel Shalem, close to Kibbutz Tirat Zvi. Not properly understanding the illegality of using metal detectors and that excavations on ancient sites should not be undertaken by amateurs, he dug into the ground using a pocket knife and uncovered the bronze torso of the Roman emperor Hadrian (now prominently displayed in the Israel Museum). It was an astounding discovery. The cuirassed bronze statue of Hadrian was probably cast in sections in Rome and brought to Palestine to be set up by the Sixth Roman Legion, whose camp was located nearby, in honor of Hadrian's visit to Palestine in 130 C.E. Tel Shalem is probably the same place as the site of Salim which was close to Aenon where John the Baptist administered special water purification rites (John 3:23).

The bronze torso of
Hadrian found at Shalem.

"He [Levanthal] hauled the dark object out of the ground and rolled it over. Looking back at him was a face. 'It seemed to be saying thanks for letting me out of the ground', he says. Levanthal rolled the head and the pipe – which turned out to be the statue's neck – in a t-shirt, strapped it down in a small duffel bag to the back of his bike and pedaled the two kilometers back to his sister's house in the religious kibbutz. 'I drank two quarts of water and went to lunch'"

(Abraham Rabinovich, "Digging up an Emperor," The Jerusalem Post, May 27, 1977).

Part Four:

THE HOLY LAND: JUDAISM AND CHRISTIANITY

Holy symbols: a carved Christian cross (*opposite*) and a Jewish candelabra.

The Land of Israel came to be known as the "Holy Land", a focus of prayers for Christians, during the Byzantine period (325-638 C.E.), namely from when Christianity was firmly established as the official religion of the Roman empire at the time of Constantine the Great. Paganism was rapidly abolished but Jewish and Samaritan worship was more or less tolerated by the authorities and they were allowed to practice their customs and maintain places of worship. Many Christian churches were constructed at the places where there were traditions associated with Jesus and his ministry, from the Church of the Nativity in Bethlehem to the Church of the Holy Sepulcher in Jerusalem. Pilgrims flocked to the Holy Land to check out "where these things were preached and done", to use the words made by one early pilgrim, Melito of Sardis,

Interior of the basilica of the Church of the Nativity. *Opposite:* a general view of the Church of the Nativity with the Judean Desert in the background.

The spot within the grotto of the Church where traditionally the Nativity is believed to have taken place (marked by the silver star). *Bottom:* a representation of the crucified Jesus from the church.

Bethlehem

According to the Gospel of Luke (2:7) Mary "laid him [baby Jesus] in a manger because there was no room for them in the inn". The inns from this period were large dwellings with animals kept in the lower parts, sometimes with a cave/store behind, and with the residential parts situated above, with rooms overlooking an external or internal courtyard. Hence, it is quite feasible imagining Mary and Joseph lodging in a cave adjacent to the manger itself. The spot of the nativity of Jesus is pointed out beneath the large Church of the Nativity in the center of Bethlehem. This building has a rock grotto where tradition places the actual birth of Jesus, marked by a silver star. The earliest remains uncovered there belong to the church that was dedicated in 339 C.E. The building that is visible today represents the church that was built at the spot by the Emperor Justinian in the mid-sixth century, and restored during later periods. Beautiful mosaics are visible beneath the wooden hatches seen in the modern floor of the church. Various other holy sites exist in the area of Bethlehem, notably the site of the Shepherd's Field within Beth Sahur to the east of the town.

The Church of the
Nativity in winter after
a fall of snow (*left*).
A statue of the Good
Shepherd (*right*).

The Greek-Orthodox site of
the Shepherd's Field. Note the
archaeological excavations in the
area in front of the modern church.

Green reeds and foliage along the Jordan River.

Baptism Sites and John the Baptist

The Jordan River has great significance for Jews as the place through which the twelve tribes of Israel passed into the Promised Land. According to the Gospels Jesus was baptized there by a remarkable man named John "the Baptist." John appears to have been attracted to this river because of its associations with the Prophet Elijah and his message was "repent, for the kingdom of heaven is at hand" (Matt. 3:2). The baptism of his followers signified the drowning of their old life and their emergence from the water into a new life. Numerous Byzantine remains have been found in the lower Jordan River region associated with John the Baptist, on the west bank at Qasr el-Yehud, and on the east bank and in the nearby Wadi Kharrar.

The Greek Orthodox monastery of Qasr el-Yehud, at the traditional baptism site in the lower Jordan Valley. *Right*: the baptism of a child at Nazareth.

"For Herod had put him [John the Baptist] to death, though he was a good man and had exhorted the Jews to lead righteous lives, to practice justice towards their fellows and piety towards God and so doing to join in baptism." (Josephus, Jewish Antiquities 116-119).

The Franciscan monastery
of St. John in the
Wilderness at Ain Habis.

In Christianity John was regarded as the forerunner of Christ. John the Baptist was apparently born in the district of Jerusalem and Byzantine tradition places his nativity at Ain Karim, a village situated west of Jerusalem. There are two ancient churches within this village, the first representing the traditional birthplace of John, and the second the place where according to tradition a meeting took place between the two mothers to be, Mary and Elizabeth (Luke 1: 41). To the west of Ain Karim is the Monastery of Ain el-Habis, or St. John in the Wilderness, with antiquities going back to Crusader times. Remarkably, in recent excavations at Suba, not far from Ain Habis, a cave was discovered with Byzantine drawings of John the Baptist and symbols of his relics on its walls. Archaeological excavations were able to show that the cave was used for baptism ceremonies already in the first century C.E., in the days of John the Baptist himself, suggesting perhaps that the reference to John spending time in "wilderness places" (Luke 1:80) may actually have had some basis in reality. Tradition places the burial of John at Sebastia, and two ancient churches dedicated to him have been uncovered at the site.

The early medieval Chapel of the Beheading of John the Baptist at Samaria (Sebastia).

The Church of the Visitation at Ain Karim.

"Brushing away the soil covering the lower part of the wall of the cave. I could not believe my eyes. 'Come and have a look at this', I shouted to Arthur, the teenager assisting me with the archaeological surveying. 'What do you make of this?' We crawled closer to the wall of the cave, wriggling past boulders with the tops of our heads brushing against the ceiling, until our faces came close to the clammy yellow cave wall. I held the torch forwards at an oblique angle to help highlight an incised image I thought I could make out on the side wall of the cave. Was this a drawing of a Roman soldier? I sensed I was on the verge of making a major archaeological discovery – I could feel tingling in my hands… It suddenly occurred to me that the large figure might be a representation of John the Baptist himself." (S. Gibson, The Cave of John the Baptist, 2004, p. 1)

An incised drawing of John the Baptist from the Byzantine period in the plaster wall of a cave at Suba close to Ain Karim. *Right*: the cave of John the Baptist at Suba.

The Church of the Annunciation at Nazareth.

Nazareth

Very little is known about the plan and appearance of Nazareth from the time of Jesus. While Jesus is said to have been born in Bethlehem and while little is known about the origins of Joseph and Mary, what is absolutely certain is that Jesus spent much of his youth living in the village of Nazareth. This town had blossomed economically on account of its proximity to the new capital city Sepphoris (Tsippori) which was being built up by Herod Antipas, tetrarch of Galilee. Local carpenters and other artisans were clearly in demand and unemployment in that region

must have been quite low at that point in time.

The large Church of the Annunciation, which dominates the modern city of Nazareth, is a modern rebuild of an ancient church dating back to the Crusader period. Some of the sculpted pieces and stone capitals were made by French artisans. Earlier remains date back to Roman and Byzantine periods. On the outskirts of Nazareth is a modern reconstruction of a first-century village, which allows visitors to experience what Nazareth might have been like at the time of Jesus.

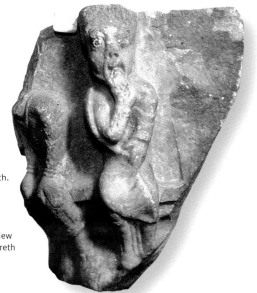

Top: A fragmentary Crusader-period carving from Nazareth. *Center*: the interior of the Church of the Annunciation with a service in progress. *Bottom*: a pastoral view on a hillside of Nazareth above the so-called "Jesus Village".

A general view of a church at Cana and the surrounding town.

"And in the sixth month the angel Gabriel was sent from God unto a city of Galilee, named Nazareth. To a virgin espoused to a man whose name was Joseph, of the house of David; and the virgin's name was Mary."

(Luke 1: 26-27).

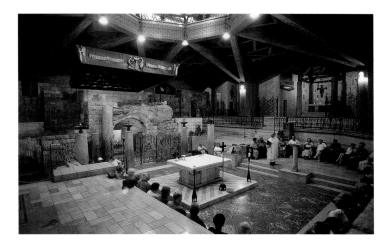

From the writings of the Piacenza Pilgrim of 570 C.E.: "In the synagogue [of Nazareth] there is kept the book in which the Lord wrote his ABC, and in this synagogue there is the bench on which he sat with the other children".

Cana

The village of Cana in the hills of Galilee was the scene of the first miracle of Jesus, the turning of water into wine during the course of a wedding (John 2: 1-11). Cana was also the headquarters of Josephus' supporters while preparations for the defenses of Galilee were being made for the war against the Romans. Today Cana is a flourishing small town with churches. Recent archaeological excavations have brought to light stone vessels dating from the first century C.E. which remind one of the reference in John 2:6 to the "six stone jars [which] were standing there [at Cana] for the Jewish rites of purification."

"…walking among the ruins of Cana one sees large massy pots of stone answering to the description of the evangelist; not preserved nor exhibited as relics, but lying about disregarded by the present inhabitants, as antiquities with the original use of which they are altogether unacquainted." (M. Russell, Palestine, or the Holy Land.

From the Earliest Period to the Present Time, 1832, p. 319).

Top: the Galilee boat being taken for conservation, encased in polyurethane
Bottom: the Galilee boat after conservation, on show at Kibbutz Ginossar.

"The great moment arrived on the eleventh day of excavation, when water was pumped into the pit surrounding the boat. As the craft began to float, a steam shovel cut through the protective dike. The boat was sailed onto the open lake and towed 500 metres north to Kibbutz Ginossar. A crane lifted it onto the shore and later placed it into a specially built pool. There the foam was laboriously stripped off, support legs constructed and the pool filled with water." (O. Cohen, "The Lifting Aspects of the Kinneret Boat.", Bulletin of the Anglo-Israel Archaeological Society 6, 1986-87, pp. 34-35).

Jesus at the Sea of Galilee

Fed from the north by the Jordan River, the Sea of Galilee is a large freshwater lake. Numerous archaeological sites are situated not only along its shores but also underwater. In January 1986 Israel was suffering from a prolonged drought which caused the level of the Sea of Galilee to recede quite dramatically. Two brothers walking along the newly-exposed western shore, close to the ancient town of Migdal, happened across the outline of a boat's hull, which was literally sticking out of the mud. Excavations proceeded immediately and the entire boat (8.2 metres long) was lifted gingerly out of the mud in a mantle of polyurethane and conveyed to Kibbutz Ginossar for conservation. Artifacts found with the boat and radiocarbon dating of wood samples indicated that the boat dated to the first century C.E. It was an exciting discovery and it made immediate headlines, journalists quickly nicknaming it the "Jesus boat." The reality however is that the boat had nothing to do with Jesus beyond the fact that it plied the Sea of Galilee around the time he was visiting the locale.

Tabgha (Heptapegon)

Anyone who loves decorative Byzantine-period mosaics will enjoy a visit to Tabgha, which abounds in mosaic floors of beauty, one of which depicting birds, lotus flowers and marsh plants, which must be one of the most beautiful uncovered in Israel.

Near the altar of the fifth-century C.E. Byzantine church is a unique mosaic rendering of two fish with a basket of loaves between them. The name Tabgha is actually a corrupted Arabic name derived from the Greek word meaning "seven springs". The main Christian tradition associated with the place is the miracle of the multiplication of the loaves and fishes (Mark 6: 30-44). It was also from this locale that Jesus went up a mountain to pray.

The Primacy Church of St. Peter on the Tabgha shore.

Egeria (late fourth century C.E.): "Not far from there [Capernaum] are some stone steps where the Lord stood. And in the same place by the sea is a grassy field with plenty of hay and many palm trees. By them are seven springs, each flowing strongly. And this is the field where the Lord fed the people with the five loaves and two fishes. In fact the stone on which the Lord placed the bread has now been made into an altar. People who go there take away small pieces of the stone to bring them prosperity, and they are very effective… Near there on a mountain is the cave to which the Saviour climbed and spoke the Beatitudes."

(J. Wilkinson, Egeria's Travels to the Holy Land, 1981, pp. 196-200).

A general view of the Church of the Fish and Loaves at Tabgha. *Bottom*: Byzantine-period mosaic floors at Tabgha depicting birds (*left*) and fishes and loaves (*right*).

Kursi

There is something extremely serene and beautiful about the landscape at Kursi, and for that reason it does not at all fit the tradition connected to this place. Accordingly, Kursi is actually an adaptation of the name Gergesa and was the scene of the stampeding Gadarene swine possessed by devils. A large monastery with a church was uncovered at the site during archaeological excavations. To the east is a chapel with a set of rooms with mosaic floors, each mysteriously containing a large natural boulder that must have had some significance in early Christian tradition – perhaps, one could speculate something to do with the stampeding swine?

"And when he was come to the other side [of the Sea of Galilee] into the country of the Gergesenes, there met him two possessed with devils, coming out of the tombs, exceedingly fierce, so that no man might pass by that way. And, behold, they cried out, saying, What have we to do with thee, Jesus, thou son of God? Art thou come hither to torment us before the time? And there was a good way off from them an herd of many swine feeding. So the devils besought him, saying, If thou cast us out, suffer us to go away into the herd of swine. And he said unto them, Go. And when they were come out, they went into the herd of swine: and, behold, the whole herd of swine ran violently down a steep place into the sea, and perished in the waters." (Matthew 8: 28-32).

The Byzantine monastery-church at Kursi (Gergesa).

A view of Bethsaida.

Bethsaida

Bethsaida was a small fisherman's village on the north-east shore of the Sea of Galilee and the home of a number of Jesus' disciples; it was also reckoned as the place where he healed the blind (Mark 8: 22). Excavations have been undertaken at the site of et-Tell – identified as ancient Bethsaida – revealing impressive Iron Age and Hellenistic remains.

The site of the Roman and Byzantine village of Capernaum, with the reconstructed synagogue in the center and the House of Peter (under cover) on the left.

Capernaum

According to the Gospels, Capernaum is where Jesus, on leaving Nazareth, began his public ministry (Matthew 4:13). Capernaum (Arabic Tel Hum, Hebrew Kefar Nahum) was an ancient fishing village on the western shore of the Sea of Galilee, with evidence of occupation going back to Hellenistic times. At the time of Jesus it may have numbered a thousand individuals, and at the time of Herod Antipas, the son of Herod the Great, it was situated within his territory. Jesus is said to have stayed in Peter's house at Capernaum, in which he taught and healed the sick. Excavations have brought to light an octagonal church of Byzantine date and beneath it remnants of first-century dwellings with small and cramped rooms, with walls built out of basalt fieldstones. An impressive synagogue also exists at the site, but it dates from a later period.

A carving from the synagogue at Capernaum (*left*), and the shore of the Sea of Galilee at Capernaum (*right*).

"And again he [Jesus] entered Capernaum after some days; and it was noised that he was in the house. And straightaway many were gathered together, insomuch that there was no room to receive them, no, not so much as about the door: and he preached the word unto them." (Mark 2: 1)

The summit of the traditional Mount of Beatitudes with the Sea of Galilee in the background.

Mount of Beatitudes

The traditional spot where Jesus delivered the Sermon on the Mount is lower down the hill, not far from Tabgha, where there are the Byzantine remains of a chapel. The new church, however, situated further up the hill, built in 1938, has a much better view of the breathtaking countryside and of the shimmering blue of the Sea of Galilee.

"And when he [Jesus] had sent them [the disciples] away, he departed into a mountain to pray." (Mark 6: 46).

Left: a place of meditation and prayer on the Mount of Beatitudes. *Right*: the hills of Galilee seen through the arches of the modern chapel on the Mount of Beatitudes.

Tiberias

Founded by Herod Antipas between 18 and 20 C.E. and named after his patron the emperor Tiberias, Josephus waxes forth enthusiastically about the beauty of some of its buildings, notably the royal palace which he says had ceilings partly covered with gold and other ornamentation with representations of animals. There are also references to royal treasure houses in the city, archives and a synagogue that Josephus states was "a huge building, capable of accommodating a large crowd." The synagogue was used for meetings and we hear of it also being used as an arena for discussing political matters. The town was situated on the shore of the Sea of Galilee, and remains of numerous buildings from the Roman and Byzantine periods have been unearthed, notably a bath-house, a marketplace, a basilica, a theater, and a stadium on the shore. On a rocky precipice west of Mount Berenice to the west of the town is a Byzantine-period church with an odd anchor-shaped stone – of some unknown religious significance – situated within the chancel area.

Top: the bath and basilica uncovered within Roman Tiberias. *Right*: a mosaic floor with a depiction of a lion.

"After these things Jesus showed himself again to the disciples at the sea of Tiberias…" (John 21: 1).

Mount Berenice with the Church of the Anchor overlooking the Sea of Galilee.

The soft pinkish-golden touch to the rooftops of Jerusalem and to the Mount of Olives during sunset.

A view of Bethany (el-Azariya) with medieval ruins in the *center* (*left*), and the Church of Gethsamene at the foot of the Mount of Olives (*right*).

Jesus' Final Days in Jerusalem

There are many Christian sites with archaeological remains in Jerusalem associated in tradition with the story of Jesus' final days. It was there Jesus publicly confronted representatives of Roman rule, on the one hand, and Jewish religious authorities on the other (Mark 11:18). Jesus first arrived from the east at the village of Bethany (Mark 11:1), known today as el-Azariya, i.e. a corruption of the name Lazarus. The Jewish Temple was his focus like the many thousands of pilgrims arriving in Jerusalem for the Passover festivities, and in the outer court he encountered the money-changers and the sellers of doves (Mark 11:15). The Gospels make it clear that Jesus had occasion to visit various private dwellings in Jerusalem. Palatial houses belonging to aristocrats and priestly families have been uncovered in the Jewish Quarter but it is unlikely Jesus frequented such homes. Jesus tended to concentrate his attention on the outsiders of society, namely those regarded as outcasts and sinners, or, alternatively, those with dubious professions such as tax-collectors and prostitutes (Mark 2:17). The areas of the Bethesda and Siloam Pools, in the New and Lower cities respectively, were therefore the areas he would have spent most of his time.

On his last night he supped with his disciples and then went to the hill of Gethsamene where he was subsequently betrayed by Judas and arrested. The remains of a first-century house with fantastic wall paintings (similar to those

"And when he [Jesus] came into Jerusalem, all the city was moved, saying. Who is this? And the multitude said, This is Jesus the prophet of Nazareth of Galilee. And Jesus went into the Temple of God, and cast out all of them that sold and bought in the Temple, and overthrew the tables of the money changers, and the seats of them that sold doves." (Matthew 21: 10-11)

Ancient gnarled olive trees at Gethsamene.

The Stone of the Anointing (of the body of Jesus) in the Church of the Holy Sepulcher.
Left: a bird's-eye view of the Church of the Holy Sepulcher and adjacent buildings in the Old City of Jerusalem.

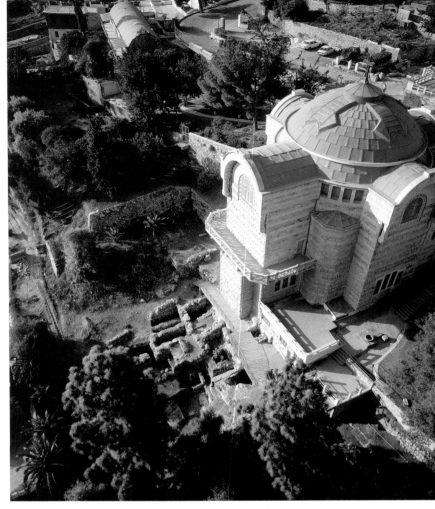

The Church of Eleona, named after Queen Helena, on the Mount of Olives.

uncovered at Pompeii) have been uncovered at the traditional spot of the house of the High Priest Caiaphas where Jesus was temporarily imprisoned before being taking to Pilate (Matthew 26: 3-5). The exact place of the trial of Jesus (Mark 15:16) is debated, but it appears to have taken place within the general area of the praetorium, the residence of the Roman prefect Pontius Pilate, and not at the Antonia Fortress. Jesus was crucified at Golgotha (Mark 15:22), a rocky knoll situated on the west side of the city near the main road. The wood for the cross, which was T-shaped in appearance, is said to have been brought from the area of the Monastery of the Cross. He was subsequently buried within a new tomb provided by Joseph of Arimathaea. Jesus would have been prepared for burial "in the manner of the Jews", wrapped in a shroud and then entombed (Mark 15:46). A tomb has recently been excavated in the nearby Akeldama cemetery with the remains of a shrouded man dating to the time of Jesus. This is the first discovery of its kind in Jerusalem. The tomb of Jesus is identified at the Church of the Holy Sepulcher (the Edicule), and the archaeological evidence that this was indeed a first-century tomb is strong. Attempts to place the tomb on the north side of the city at the Garden Tomb and to the east on the Mount of Olives are without foundation.

The location of the tomb was distinctly preserved in the memory of the populace, notwithstanding the fact that Hadrian later built a temple or shrine to Venus over it. Subsequently Constantine the Great had a large martyrium built next to the Tomb of Jesus and leading from the main street of the city (the Cardo). In a deep pit in the ground Constantine's mother Helena was said to have found fragments of the discarded true cross. Tucked away in one corner of the excavations behind the Chapel of St. Helena is a votive stone with a drawing of a Roman ship and a Latin inscription Domine Ivimus ("Lord, we went").

A coin bearing a portrait of Queen Helena, mother of Constantine the Great (*left*), and a second-century drawing of a Roman merchantman in the Church of the Holy Sepulcher with a Latin inscription reading *Domine Ivimus* (Lord, we went) (*right*).

The Greek Orthodox Monastery of the Cross, with housing of modern Jerusalem in the background

Emmaus

After the crucifixion of Jesus, two of his disciples who were on the highway leading from Jerusalem westwards encountered a man whom they later realized was the risen Christ (Luke 24: 13 ff.). Some scholars have identified this Emmaus with Emmaus-Nicopolis (Imwas in Arabic), close to Latrun, but the great distance from Jerusalem suggests that it might have been at Emmaus-Colonia at Motza, a walking distance from Jerusalem, instead. Archaeological excavations have taken place at both locations bringing to light an array of remains dating from Neolithic through medieval times.

"And behold, two of them [the disciples] went that same day to a village called Emmaus, which was from Jerusalem about threescore furlongs. And they talked together of all these things which had happened. And it came to pass, that, while they communed together and reasoned, Jesus himself drew near, and went with them." (Luke 24: 13-15).

The ruins of the church and monastery at Emmaus, near Latrun.

Legio

It's not exactly the sort of place where one would think of doing scientific digging – in a jailhouse – but this is where rescue excavations brought to light a remarkable find: a ceremonial Christian meeting hall, dating from the 3rd century C.E. The workforce for the dig consisted of the Megiddo Jail inmates: Jews, Moslems, Christians and Druze. Most of them, I suppose, would have liked to burrow an escape route out of the jail, but many of them, it appears, came to enjoy the experience of studying the ancient past. A large mosaic floor was found bearing geometric designs, a medallion with fish, and three Greek inscriptions: one mentioning a Roman soldier of centurion-rank who donated towards the cost of the mosaic, the second a dedication in the memory of four female dignitaries, and the third a reference to a lady who dedicated an offering table to Christ.

An exquisite bird's-eye view of a mosaic floor uncovered in the Megiddo Jail. Note the medallion with a depiction of fish (left) and the adjoining Greek dedicatory inscriptions.

A bird's-eye view of the monastery at Mar Saba, showing the church (marked by the blue domes) and the tomb of Sabas (the building with the red dome).

Byzantine Monasteries

Between the 4th and 8th centuries C.E. numerous monasteries sprung up in different parts of the Holy Land and particularly in the desert regions of Judea. Judean Desert monks tended to quote the call to Abraham: "Get thee out of thy country, and from thy kindred, and from thy father's house, unto a land that I shall show thee." They saw themselves as the successors of the Hebrew prophets, practicing asceticism and abstinence. The desert was the best location. "The Desert a City" is the apt title of a book about ancient monasticism by Derwas J. Chitty. There were two types of monasteries: the monastery of the hermit (*lavra*) and the communal monastery (*coenobium*). Numerous excavations have been undertaken at ruined Judean Desert monasteries, such as at Khan el-Ahmar and Ma'ale Edumim. Some monasteries, notably those of Mar Saba, St. George's, and Theodosius, are still maintained by monks. Ancient monasteries are known from other parts of the Holy Land as well, with a monastery excavated at Tel Beth Shemesh in the early twentieth century by Duncan MacKenzie. Within the modern city of nearby Beth Shemesh, a recent excavation has brought to light a monastery at Khirbet es-Suyyagh.

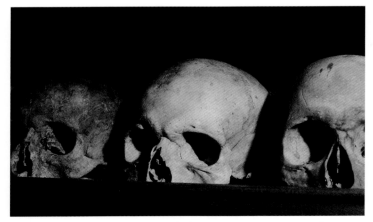

The stacked-up skulls of deceased monks (*left*), and one of the interior rooms of a monastery (*right*).

A general view of the Mar Saba monastery, situated in the wilderness east of Bethlehem.

The monastery of Qarantal above Jericho (the fortress of Dok was situated on top of the hill).

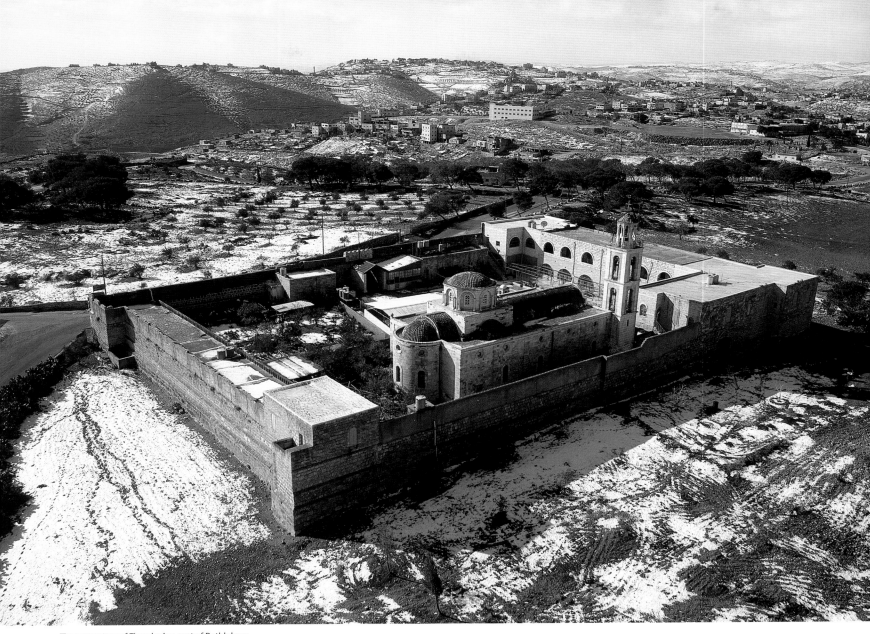

The monastery of Theodosius east of Bethlehem.

"The abbot Anthony said: 'Fish, if they tarry on dry land, die: even so monks that tarry outside their cell or abide with men of the world fall away from their vow of quiet. As a fish must return to the sea, so must we to our cell: lest it befall that by tarrying without, we forget the watch within.'" (Helen Waddell, The Desert Fathers, 1965, p. 81)

An interior view of a monastery still in use (*left*), and the Maale Edumim monastery excavations in the Judean Desert, now surrounded by modern buildings (*right*).

Left and right: the Monastery of St. George in the Wadi Kelt.

Center left: a Byzantine-period painting of holy men from Caesarea.
Right: the Monastery at Khan el-Ahmar. *Bottom left:* a holy book from
a monastery. *Bottom right:* the Monastery at Tel Beth Shemesh.

Byzantine Towns in the Negev

The efflorescence of settlement in the Negev Desert occurred in the Byzantine period from the 4th century C.E., with the strengthening and enlarging of the former Roman towns, with the construction of numerous churches, and the consolidation of the agricultural hinterland by the construction of complex field and terrace systems. The key towns of this period are situated at Avdat, Haluza, Mampsis, Rehovot-in-the-Negev, Shivta and Nessana.

A sundial found during excavations at Mampsis.

A general view of the acropolis at Avdat.

Avdat

Avdat (Oboda) may have had some 500 dwellings according to one of the excavators of the site. These were situated on the west slope beneath the acropolis area and comprised small stone structures with caves behind. On top of the acropolis two churches and a baptistery were constructed. An inscription identifies the southern church as the Martyrion of St. Theodore.

"It is an eye-opening experience to visit the still extant ruins of the main Byzantine cities in the Negev. The despoiled wreckage of their above-surface remains testifies eloquently to the nature of their former grandeur. It appears, at first, impossible to understand how such large urban centers could have existed in view of the bleakness and emptiness of their present surroundings. It takes time and patience to perceive how large groups of human beings could live permanently off a land, which seems superficially to be so ill favored." (Nelson Glueck, Rivers in the Desert, 1968, p. 257).

A view of the narthex of a church at Avdat. *Bottom:* the theatre uncovered in Haluza.

Haluza

Correctly identifying the ruins as ancient Elusa
on account of its Arabic name el-Khalasa, Edward
Robinson first visited the site during his extensive
tour of the country in 1838. The largest church yet
discovered in the Negev was uncovered at Haluza
during archaeological excavations. Large and well-built
steps led to the chancel and to the bishop's throne
located beneath the central apse. Three other churches
are known to have existed at the site.

175

Mampsis

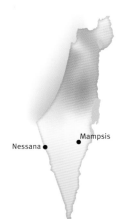

One of the important Byzantine towns of the Negev, Mampsis (Hebrew Mamshit), was first seen in 1838 by the American scholar Edward Robinson through binoculars but since the site seemed to him to be such a maze of ruins he decided not to descend the mountain to investigate it. This was his loss, since the site has remarkable archaeological remains dating back to the time of the Nabateans, as well as major buildings from the Byzantine period. The Christians who lived in this town were hemmed in by the constricted plan of the original settlement, which meant that by squeezing in two churches, some earlier buildings and a section of the fortification wall were razed. In one of the tombs in the Mampsis cemetery was a hoard of 30 clay seal impressions (*bullae*), one of which was a copy of a coin of Hadrian from 130 C.E. Other seal impressions bore the images of a scorpion and a centaur.

Top: a view of the ruins at Mampsis. *Center*: a mosaic floor depicting peacocks flanking an amphora, and (*left*) Clay seal impressions. *Bottom*: the large church at Mampsis.

Nessana

During the 1935-36 Colt expedition to the site of Nessana (Auja Hafir), excavators discovered an amazing cache of several hundred papyri written in Greek, Latin, Aramaic, Syriac and Arabic. One record (No. 89), described by the translator as a "dry little record," actually deals with a journey that was made to a "holy mountain," presumably Mount Sinai, and includes a wealth of information on transactions that were made regarding animals, commodities and child slaves. At the end of the document the writer inserted a short prayer asking for the intercession of "Our Lady Mary Mother of God and Ever Virgin and of John the Baptist, and of all the holy saints."

The site is one of the most impressive archaeological sites in the Negev, notwithstanding the remark made by Colt before he began digging that "qualified critics had in fact declared it the worst site in the whole region." The discovery of the papyri was almost like a prize for Colt, having suffered so many calamities at Shivta, the previous site he had been excavating. Nessana started out as a Nabatean town but it was abandoned in 106 C.E. when Arabia was annexed by the Romans. The town was rebuilt substantially during the Byzantine period. Recent excavations have brought to light numerous churches and buildings. Many sculpted pieces, numerous *ostraca* (inscribed potsherds) and one or two unusual objects have been found (including a doll).

One of the churches uncovered at Nessana with the acropolis of the site visible in the background. *Bottom*: a toy doll uncovered at the site.

On the discovery of the cache of papyri: "At the instance of discovery it happened that no member of staff was at the scene. I myself was on another part of the mound and the first news I had was when an Arab boy came plunging down the hill toward me, excitedly waving a large sheet of papyrus, from which the breeze was whipping a flutter of small fragments."

(H. Dunscombe Colt, "Who Read Vergil in Zin?", The Classical Journal XLII, 6, 1947, p. 318).

On the occasion of Palmer and Drake's visit to the site in 1870: "While Drake was photographing and I myself was sketching at the fiskiyeh, some of the bloodthirsty Arabs, against whom [the guide] Suleiman had warned us, appeared in the shape of two little Arab children with topknots, who ran away screaming horribly with fright at the sight of us. An Arab lady watched the camera at a safe distance, evidently expecting it to go off. Our appearance, and the stories propogated by our worthy guides, seemed to have stricken terror into the hearts of the community."

(E. H. Palmer, "The Desert of Tih and the Country of Moab", Palestine Exploration Fund Quarterly Statement, 1871, p. 26).

A decorated lintel with a Greek inscription.

Shivta

Whatever archaeologists did at Shivta (Sbeita), things went wrong. It seemed as if the site was cursed. When Shivta, in the central western Negev, was excavated by H. Dunscombe Colt in the 1930's, he and his team suffered a series of natural calamities, beginning with a sandstorm and ending with a major drought. Colt and his colleagues were disappointed with their findings ("confidentially, our discoveries failed to shake the archaeological world") and morale remained low. Yet another calamity fell upon the excavators in 1938 when the dig-house was burned to the ground by rioters from Jerusalem, destroying also Colt's bright yellow model T-Ford car. Most unfortunate, however, was the destruction of archaeological artifacts and dig records.

Shivta was a very large Christian town in the Byzantine period, with a plan consisting of a few buildings (mainly churches) and many dwellings subdivided by a seemingly-haphazard network of narrow streets and alleyways. Rainwater was collected in large reservoirs and cisterns, and terraced field systems existed in the nearby valleys.

A decorated lintel of a doorway leading into a church at Shivta.

A general view of the site and of the principal church.

"For a week we prospected contently for a likely place to start. At the end of that week a sandstorm came up at midnight and blew all our tents down, and we spent the rest of the night clinging to our more volatile possessions. In the grim light of dawn we agreed to take up residence in a more sheltered refuge. The cook-tent, dining-tent and store-tent found sanctuary in the bottom of a large ancient reservoir in the centre of the ruins; the rest of us picked out likely house walls and pitched our tents in their lee."

(H. Dunscombe Colt, "Who Read Vergil in Zin?", The Classical Journal XLII, 6, 1947, p. 316)

Byzantine tombstone inscribed in Greek found at the site: "Fell asleep Jacob, the thrice-blessed priest, on the 24th of the month Hyperberetaios, the year 425"

(Y. Tsafrir, Excavations at Rehovot-in-the-Negev. Vol. 1, 1988, p. 155).

Right: the chancel area of the church uncovered at Rehovot-in-the-Negev. *Center*: some of the column shafts and bases from the site.

Rehovot-in-the-Negev

Situated in the heart of the Negev Desert next to a well-trodden track, Rehovot-in-the-Negev (or Khirbet Ruheibeh in Arabic) has yielded rich archaeological finds, particularly from the Roman and Byzantine periods. The site was distinguished by a bathhouse, which was destroyed by the Turks in the First World War to make way for a police post. Recent excavations brought to light the North Church with a well preserved crypt with walls faced with marble. An exciting discovery was of small glass plaques decorated with images of saints. The cemetery yielded many epitaphs dating from 536 to 601 C.E.

Desert Agriculture in the Negev

It was once thought that the Nabateans were the ones who introduced wide-scale agricultural terracing into the Negev Desert, owing to their major interest in water collection and conservation procedures. However, the Nabateans were much more interested in the caravan routes across the region, and their Negev towns served as trading posts rather than as agricultural centers. Archaeological research has shown that the terracing seen across wide areas of the Negev was first created in the Byzantine period and was maintained and enlarged quite substantially during the Umayyad period, with the building of numerous farms. Very early examples of open-air mosques and numerous rock inscriptions in *kufic* Arabic have also been found.

Terraced fields in the Negev Desert.

179

Ancient Synagogues in the Galilee

The destruction of the Jewish Temple in Jerusalem by the Romans in 70 C.E. was a calamitous event for the Jewish people. Not long after this event a different, alternative form of worship and liturgy began within purposeful structures known as synagogues (Hebrew bet ha-knesset). Although such buildings already existed in the first century C.E., in view of the content of the Theodotos inscription from Jerusalem (see above, p. 89), and in light of the discovery of stepped assembly buildings at Masada, Gamla, Herodium, Modi'in, Horvat Etri and elsewhere, they may very well have served civic, schooling and everyday functions, as well as having being used for worship. Numerous religious synagogue buildings dating from the Byzantine period, with early examples from the 4th/5th centuries C.E., notably the basilical type of synagogues, have been found in the Holy Land, with a marked concentration in the north of the country. Capernaum is an excellent example of an early synagogue, and when it was first visited by Edward Robinson in 1838 he thought it

The synagogue at Hamath Tiberias.

might actually be a heathen temple or church instead, but revised his opinion during a later visit in 1852. Some of the later examples of synagogues, which begin in the 5th century and continue to exist, at least in some cases, until the 7th/8th centuries, have ornate mosaic floors, Hebrew inscriptions and a *bema*. Various symbols, such as the candelabra (*menorah*), the *shofar* and the shovel appear as prominent motifs in mosaic floors, on capitals and other wall decorations. A good example of a later synagogue comes from Hamath Tiberias, situated close to hot springs, next to the Sea of Galilee.

Capernaum before excavations were commenced at the site. *Left*: a general view of the synagogue of Capernaum today.

Lieutenant Samuel Anderson lecturing in 1867 about the work of Charles Wilson at Capernaum: "At the ruins of Tell Hum, on the north-west shore of the lake, a synagogue was excavated, and the plan of the building was completely disclosed. The massive blocks of limestone used in the building are of such hard material as to be susceptible of a hard polish, but most of the stones have been carried away at different times to be built into new buildings in Tiberias."

(PEF Proceedings and Notes, Meeting at Cambridge, 8 May, 1867, p. 9)

Kefar Baram

There are two synagogues at Kefar Baram, one small and the other large. The large one is fairly well preserved and has many visitors; it has an impressive façade and its doorways are intact, with a columned vestibule in front. It was used for dwelling purposes until the twentieth century, which explains why it escaped destruction. The small synagogue was recorded by the explorers Charles Wilson and Herbert Kitchener in the nineteenth century, and its whereabouts were lost until recently when new excavations revealed its foundations once again. Unfortunately, the lintel of the large doorway bearing the two lambs in relief and an inscription in Hebrew was destroyed almost completely in the 1890s. It read: "Peace be upon this place and upon all the places of Israel. Joseph the Levite the son of Levi put up this lintel. A blessing rest upon this work." Professor Sukenik (father of Yigal Yadin), while visiting the site in 1929, sadly reported that "a fragment of one of the doorposts…was still lying near this spot on my visit there…"

A general view of the large synagogue at Kefar Baram. *Bottom*: the façade of the large synagogue.

The Synagogue of Kefar Baram, according to Rabbi Jacob (1238-1244) was: "a beautiful building made of large stones and long pillars. No man ever saw a building as beautiful as that."

"In the fields to the north of the village there was until recently a very striking doorway belonging to a second smaller synagogue. It is figured in the PEF memoirs and when I visited the place in 1893 it was still standing. In 1907 I found it gone and learned that the magnificent sculptured monolith of which it was composed had been thrown down and cut up for building stones."

(E.W.G. Masterman, Studies in Galilee, 1909, pp. 117-118).

A mosaic panel from Beth Shean depicting an *aedicule* flanked by candelabra (*menorot*) with the *shofar* and shovel.

Horvat Shema'

Situated close to the foot of the impressive Mount Meiron in the Upper Galilee was a small village, and within its cramped confines was a synagogue with an unusual plan, dating to the 4th-5th centuries C.E. A room with wall paintings at the far end of the building may have housed a portable shrine to contain the holy writings (Torah). The final phase of the synagogue was destroyed in an abrupt earthquake. Archaeologists uncovered signs of absolute devastation. Tumbled and shattered stone debris was found throughout the building. The inhabitants fled for their lives and the synagogue was never rebuilt.

On an earthquake in the Galilee in 1837: "As far as the eye can reach, nothing is seen but one vast chaos of stones and earth, timber and boards, tables, chairs, beds and clothing, mingled in horrible confusion. Men everywhere at work, worn out and wo-begone, uncovering their houses in search of the mangled and putrified bodies of departed friends..."

(E. Robinson, Biblical Researches in Palestine, Vol. 3, 1841, p. 472).

Top and bottom: general views of the ancient synagogues at Horvat Shema' and Gush Halav.

Gush Halav

Overlooking a green and fertile valley beneath the Christian Maronite village of el-Jish (Gush Halav, literally "milk lump") in the Upper Galilee, are the remains of a stone-built synagogue with its main entrance facing south towards Jerusalem. On one of the fallen columns was a Hebrew inscription reading: "José son of Tanhum made this shrine. Let him be blessed." We can only hope he was.

"New data brings new insights. While the material from Gush Halav alters somewhat the older views, it underscores the capacity of an individual religious community for originality within certain parameters. The overall architectural forms, however immersed within the Greco-Roman provincial world they may be, reflect a looseness and freedom from rigidity that is refreshing to the student of Roman provincial art."

(E. Meyers and J. F. Strange, Archaeology, the Rabbis and Early Christianity, 1981, p. 147)

The synagogue at Meroth.

Meroth

Clearing away the soil very carefully, archaeologists working at Meroth (Marus) were pleasantly surprised to find a highly colorful mosaic floor depicting a young warrior (possibly King David) surrounded by a sword, helmet and shield (perhaps the weapons captured from Goliath). The Aramaic inscription next to it bears the name of one of the benefactors: "Yodan Bar Shimon Mani". The synagogue itself was built late in the 4th century or early in the 5th century C.E. Next to the building a carved lintel was found and along its bottom edge was an Aramaic version of the verse from Deuteronomy (28:6): "Blessed shalt thou be when thou comest in, and blessed shalt thou be when thou goest out", which is

a most appropriate inscription to find over a doorway. Next to the synagogue a bronze amulet was also found bearing a 26-line appeal to God from a certain Yossie, son of Zenovia, asking for authority over the village. Whether or not he was granted his wish we shall probably never know.

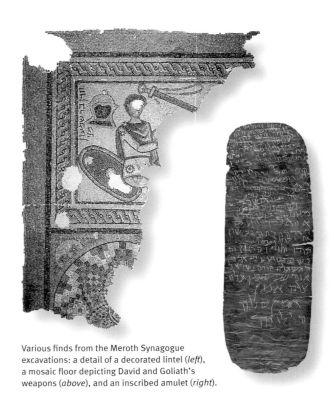

Various finds from the Meroth Synagogue excavations: a detail of a decorated lintel (*left*), a mosaic floor depicting David and Goliath's weapons (*above*), and an inscribed amulet (*right*).

The synagogue at Chorazin. *Below*: a decorated pediment made from basalt from the synagogue .

Chorazin

Chorazin (Kerazeh) was a small village in the hills overlooking the Sea of Galilee which came to be reproached by Jesus: "Woe unto thee Chorazin! Woe unto thee Bethsaida! For if the mighty works had been done in Tyre and Sidon, which have been done in you, they had a great while ago repented, sitting in sackcloth and ashes." (Luke 10:13). Excavations revealed the remains of the synagogue built of local black basalt and some of the local houses, including one with an oil press. A number of architectural fragments of exquisite beauty were found, as well as a few sculpted pieces representing lions, and a basalt seat which may have been a "Throne of Moses" used during the reading of the holy writings (Torah).

"Anderson, during his topographical rambles, has made a great discovery, no less than the ruins of Chorazin at Kerazeh… A curious tongue or projection runs out in the wady, and on this, which commands a beautiful view of the lake, are the remains of a synagogue or church, perhaps both. Unfortunately, though some of the mouldings, &c., are in a good state, the building has suffered more than any of the others, and its plan cannot be distinctly made out. All the buildings, including synagogue, are of basalt, and it is not till one is right in amongst them that one sees clearly what they are; 50 or 100 yards off they look nothing more than the rough heaps of basaltic stones so common in this country. Portions of the old streets, with their pavements, can be traced, and there is a great deal of broken pottery lying about."

(Letter III of Charles Wilson of 20th January 1866, in PEF Proceedings and Notes, p.30)

Reconstructed columns in the synagogue.

Meiron

The synagogue at Meiron is a good example of a synagogue which has suffered the ravages of time quite substantially, yet enough of it has survived to indicate its former glory. The building was first excavated in 1866 by the intrepid explorer Charles Wilson, but he found little of it was preserved except for the façade with its three entrances. A picture taken by his photographer, Henry Phillips, shows that an entire cornice was preserved immediately above the lintel of the main door. It also appears in a sketch made by one of the team members of the Survey of Western Palestine in 1877, but very little of this cornice has been preserved in modern times, and recently even these few remaining stones disappeared forever. Luckily we have Phillip's original photograph.

Top and center: the synagogue façade at Meiron.

"The principal of sacred orientation may be observed in the basilical structure found in the American excavations at ancient Meiron, where the triple façade faces south toward Jerusalem. It has hitherto been assumed that in a basilical synagogue of this kind the ark was not yet a permanent fixture but a portable structure wheeled out during worship into the main sanctuary." (E. Meyers and J. F. Strange, Archaeology, the Rabbis and Early Christianity, 1981, p. 147)

Arbel

The location of the synagogue at Arbel (Irbid) is at a spot of great beauty, overlooking the cliffs where, according to the first-century writer Josephus Flavius, Herod the Great fought Jewish insurgents hiding in the caves. Edward Robinson, who saw the synagogue at Irbid in 1852, was overcome with excitement and wrote that it was "the remains of a single edifice. This was a Jewish structure, precisely in the same style of Jewish architecture that we had seen at Kefr Bir'im [Kefar Baram] and Meiron. There is a portal with sculptured ornaments towards the east. One of the interior columns is standing, and there is also a fine Corinthian capital."

In 1210 Rabbi Samuel Ben Samson wrote: "we climbed to Arbela, where stood the great synagogue which Nittai caused to be built there; it is now, on account of our sins, in ruins. It lies in the centre of the town."

The synagogue at Arbel.

Synagogues of the Golan

Katzrin
Kanaf
Um el-Kanatir

The remains of about 25 synagogues, dating from the 5th-6th centuries C.E., have been found in the Golan Heights, with archaeological excavations conducted at Katzrin, En Nashut, Horvat Kanaf, Deir Aziz and Um el-Kanatir. As the principal public building they dominated the villages in which they were located. Built of blocks of basalt, they had thick walls, ornamental doorways, internal benches and columned interiors. At Deir Aziz, where a Greek inscription "Azizo" was found, which perhaps indicates the original name of the village, an apse-like *bema* was found for the ark in the southern wall. Another site, Um el-Kanatir (which is Arabic for "rich in arches"), was first investigated by Schumacher in the nineteenth century and he described the synagogue as concealed by gigantic piles of hewn stones. These stones were

recently digitally recorded using the most advanced photographic means available and then removed one-by-one using a special mechanical lifting device specially prepared for the site. A computerized log was made of every single stone excavated at the site.

"Following the recording, the architectural elements are numbered and an electronic chip is inserted into each one of them. The chip has a unique number which links it to a data-base, which has all the data about the stone with the addition of a plan and a record, thus allowing the reader to draw out the specific ID of the stone and perhaps also to ascertain its position within the future reconstruction."

(Y. Drey, H. Ben David, and I. Gonen, "The Synagogue of Um el-Kanatir: From the 5th to the 21st Centuries", in U. Livner ed., Advances in the Study of the Ancient Synagogue and its World, 2004, p. 5)

Top: basalt slab with nine-stemmed *menorah*, *shofar*, and shovel. *Bottom*: the main entrance leading into the Katzrin synagogue with a lintel decorated with a wreath. *opposite:* A general view of the Katzrin synagogue and the surrounding ancient village.

The ruined synagogue of Horvat Kanaf (the structure behind is modern) with scattered architectural fragments made of basalt.

The synagogue of Um el-Kanatir under excavation (*left*) and a fragment of a decorated arch made of basalt (*right*).

Theodoret of Cyrrhus (c. 393-466 C.E.): "Through Moses the God of all gave this language, not natural but acquired by learning. For while all others speak the language of the people among whom they are born… as for the children of the Hebrews there is not one to be found using from the beginning the Hebrew language, but rather that of the surrounding population. Then as adolescents they learn the shape of the letters…"

(Quaestiones in Genesin IX-X, Qu. 61, Migne, Pat. Gr. LXXX, 165).

The excavated ruins of a synagogue at Deir Aziz (*top* and *center*).

The interior of the En Nashut synagogue (*left*), and an adjacent oil press (*right*).

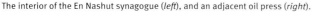

189

The Susiya synagogue after a fall of snow (*left*), and the excavations of the adjacent village (*right*).

Synagogues of the South

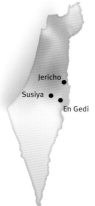

Synagogues, while extremely prevalent in the north of the country, are also known in other regions as well, notably at Susiya, Eshtemoa, Horvat Maon and Anim in the southern Judean Hills, and at En Gedi on the western shore of the Dead Sea. The Susiya synagogue was graced with beautiful mosaic floors and stone carvings, one of which is a lintel with a depiction of the Jewish candelabra (*menorah*). An inscription from the site has dates counted according to Sabbatical years and also from the time of the Creation of the World. The excavation of the En Gedi synagogue brought to light a variety of rich finds, including a hoard of 6000 coins mysteriously hidden beneath the niche where the Ark of the Law the mosaic floors of the synagogue, one containing curses against those who commit sins. Recent excavations have brought to light the remains of a village in the vicinity of the synagogue, probably the same one referred to by Eusebius as "a very large village of Jews" (*Onom.* 86:16).

A mosaic floor depicting animals. *Opposite*: a mosaic floor from a synagogue at Jericho showing a *menorah* (candelabrum) flanked by a *lulav* and *shofar* and with a Hebrew inscription reading "Peace on Israel".

The village at En Gedi with the remains of the synagogue protected under the tent-like structure.

En Gedi Synagogue inscription: "…Anyone causing a controversy between a man and his friend, or whoever slanders his friend before the Gentiles, or whoever reveals the secret of the town to the Gentiles — He whose eyes range through the whole earth and Who sees hidden things, He will set his face on that man and on his seed and will uproot him from under the heavens. And all the people said: Amen and Amen Selah."

A general view of Beth Shearim with the main entrance into the subterranean necropolis seen center left.

In regard to the burial place of Rabbi Judah Ha-Nassi we are told: "Rabbi [Judah] lies [sick] at Sepphoris and a [burial] place is prepared for him at Beth Shearim… Rabbi was [living] at Beth Shearim, but because he took sick they took him to Sepphoris, which is high and its air perfumed." (Ketuboth 103b)

Beth Shearim

Beth Shearim was an important center of Jewish learning as rabbinical writings attest. It was there that Rabbi Judah Ha-Nassi, editor of the Mishna, established the seat of the Sanhedrin. Rabbi Judah was interred there, and subsequently numerous Jews chose to be buried there as well. Archaeological excavations within the thirty or so rock-cut catacombs at Beth Shearim brought to light numerous sarcophagi, inscriptions and incised and carved Jewish symbols, including representations of the candelabra (*menorah*), Ark of the Law, *lulav, shofar, ethrog*, as well as drawings of ships and horsemen. Marble fragments of broken sarcophagi were also found bearing mythological and pagan scenes, such as the one representing the myth of Leda and the Swan, but these were undoubtedly brought to this area as part of some later industrial activity, perhaps lime burning, and did not originate within the Jewish tombs.

Sarcophagus fragment depicting a mythological pagan scene of Leda and the Swan. *Below*: a *menorah* carved into one of the walls.

Center: the interior of one of the burial vaults, with a *menorah* (candelabrum) carved into one of the walls, not long after the excavations had been completed. *Bottom*: excavations of the Beth Shearim settlement.

Part Five:

ISLAM AND THE CRUSADERS

With the Islamic invasion of 638 C.E. gradual changes took place within the material culture of the land. The Umayyads were not interested in destroying in their wake but, instead, believed in maintaining local social, institutional and architectural trends that were already apparent in late Byzantine times. Many archaeological remains from this early phase of the Islamic period have been found: fortresses, desert-castles and fortified towns with dwellings, shops and pottery kilns. Roads were repaired as a number of milestones testify. A Greek inscription from Hamath Gader indicates that the local baths were rebuilt at the behest of the local Arab governor in 662 C.E. The Abbasid period also saw a renewed burst of material and architectural activity in the land, notwithstanding the major earthquake that occurred in 749 C.E.

A plaster fragment of a soldier
from Hisham's Palace near Jericho

Jerusalem and the Haram al-Sharif

The Dome of the Rock (Qubbat al-Sakhra) is undoubtedly the jewel of Islamic architecture in Jerusalem. Begun in 688 C.E. at the instigation of the Umayyad Caliph Abd al-Malik, it took three years to complete. On the south side of the Haram al-Sharif is the mosque of al-Aqsa, which was built in 705-15 C.E., replacing a simple wooden structure that Caliph Omar had set up following the surrender of the city in 638 C.E. Beneath the Dome of the Rock is an expanse of rock with a cave beneath.

Top: a gold Islamic coin from excavations in Jerusalem. *Right*: View of the Haram al-Sharif to the west at sunset. The gold dome of the Dome of the Rock is visible center right, with the silver dome of the Aqsa Mosque extreme left. *Bottom*: the interior of the Dome of the Rock showing the holy rock (sakhra).

In 1864 Charles Wilson examined the floor of the cave beneath the Dome of the Rock and wrote: "…on tapping the sides a hollow sound is produced, which the Muslims bring forward as proof of their legend that the rock is suspended in the air, but after careful examination and trying places where no hollow could exist, it was found to derive from defective plastering…" (C. W. Wilson, Ordnance Survey of Jerusalem, 1866, p. 34).

196

'Ali of Heart visiting Jerusalem in 1173 C.E. wrote: "Underneath the rock is the Cave of the Souls. They say that Allah will bring together the souls of all True Believers to this spot. You descend to this cave by some fourteen steps, and they state the grave of Zakariyya – peace be upon him – is here in this cave. The Cave of the Souls is the height of a man."

(G. Le Strange, Palestine Under the Muslims, 1890, p. 132).

The Dome of the Rock. *Right and top*: two decorated wooden ceiling panels from the Aqsa Mosque.

The Haram al-Sharif looking towards the north, with the Aqsa Mosque and the Dome of the Rock behind. In the foreground are the excavated remains of Umayyad-period palaces.

Ramla

The town was founded in 712-715 C.E. as a new city on sand dunes, hence its name Ramla (from the Arabic word for sand *ruml*). Recent archaeological excavations have indeed brought to light patches of yellow sand beneath the earliest archaeological remains from the Abbasid period. Various archaeological discoveries pertaining to the earliest town have been uncovered, notably a mosque, dwellings with numerous plastered installations, and mosaic floors, together with large amounts of artistic objects, pottery and coins. The White Mosque has an inscription indicating that the impressive tower was built in 1318 by a Mamluk sultan, but evidence provided in the sources indicates that the mosque goes back in time well before that.

Top and bottom: the White Mosque with adjacent excavated remains in Ramla.

Mukaddasi (10th century C.E.): "Ar Ramlah is the capital of Palestine. It is a fine city and well-built; its water is good and plentiful; its fruits are abundant. It combines manifold advantages, situated as it is in the midst of beautiful villages and lordly towns, near to holy places and pleasant hamlets. Commerce here is prosperous, and the markets excellent. There is no finer mosque in Islam than the one in this city. The bread is of the best and the whitest..."

Hisham's Palace

The heat was intense and we drove slowly down the dusty road north of Jericho towards the site of "Hisham's Palace" (Khirbet el-Mefjer). The site is of an Umayyad desert-castle (*qasr* in Arabic; similar in function to a European *chateau*) but it was apparently built not by Caliph Hisham, even though a plaster statue of him was found at the site. Rather, it was built by his successor designate, Walid ibn Yazid (c. 743 C.E.), who was banished from court on account of his wild living and drinking, though he was also an accomplished poet and marksman. The gate to the site was closed and padlocked, and a Palestinian guard came out of the little room built next to the main entrance. "Sorry", he said, "but we are all on strike and cannot allow visitors in." He added optimistically: "perhaps next week we will open." We took a few photographs across the wall and drove away, sad that we hadn't been given a chance to see the wonderful archaeological remains at the site. I had been to the site before, but many years ago, and having read an article by the excavator, Robert Hamilton, who described how Walid ibn Yazid occasionally bathed in wine, I wanted to see the actual bath with my own eyes.

Two plaster figures from the excavations: one of Caliph Walid depicted on a lion pedestal (*left*), and the other of a naked woman.

The rooms surrounding a large courtyard within the palace (*left*) and a star-like window feature reconstructed at the site (*right*).

The story of the singer 'Utarrad: "I was brought in to him [Walid ibn Yazid], and he was sitting in his palace (qasr) *on the edge of a small pool, just large enough for a man to turn around in when immersed; it was lined with lead and filled with wine. I had hardly time to give him the greeting when he said: 'Are you 'Utarrad?' 'Yes, Commander of the Faithful', said I. 'I have been longing to hear you'. Said he. 'Now sing to me…' So I sang it to him. I had barely finished when, by God, he tore apart an embroidered robe that was on him, worth I know not what, flung it down in two pieces, and plunged naked as his mother bore him into that pool; whence he drank, I swear, until the level was distinctly lowered. Then he was pulled out, laid down dead to the world, and covered up. So I got up and took the robe; and no one, by God, said to me 'take it' or 'leave it'. So I went to my lodging, amazed to see the liveliness of his mind and the violence of his emotion".* (R. W. Hamilton, "Who Built Khirbat al Mafjar?", Levant 1 [1969], p. 67).

Top: a fortified palatial estate at Khirbet el-Minya, with the Sea of Galilee in the background. Bottom: a gateway at Khirbet el-Minya *(left)*, and *(right)* a mosaic floor with geometric designs.

Minya, Ashdod Yam and Habonim

Another palatial estate existed at Khirbet el-Minya, not in the desert but close to Tiberias (Tabariya) which was the Umayyad capital of the *jund* of al-Urdunn. Estates of this kind were composed of baths, reception-halls and bedrooms, and were surrounded by walls with gates and towers which were built more for decoration than for defense purposes. Fortified estates have also been excavated along the Mediterranean coast at Ashdod Yam and Habonim (Kafr Lam), and based on architectural features their construction might very well have been influenced by the North African *ribats*.

Habonim (*top*) and Ashdod-Yam (*bottom*).

Top: view of mosque before and (*bottom*) after the recent excavations at Neby Samwil. *Right*: Neby Samwil following a fall of snow.

Crusaders in the Holy Land

Although Pope Urban II had already called in 1095 for the formation of an army to come to the aid of Christian communities suffering under Muslim rule, it was only during the following year that a professional army led by Raymond of St Gilles, Godrey of Bouillon, and others, set out in 1096 to the Middle East, eventually reaching Antioch. Following the capture of Antioch, the army marched on Jerusalem which was captured following a short siege on 15 July 1099.

Salah-ed-Din (Saladin) on the Crusaders: "Regard the Franj! Behold with what obstinacy they fight for their religion, while we, the Muslims, show no enthusiasm for waging holy war."

(A. Maalouf, The Crusades Through Arab Eyes, 1984, p. 1).

Neby Samwil

This was the place where the Crusaders caught their first distant glimpse of the Holy City of Jerusalem in 1099, hence the name of the place – *Mons Gaudii* (Mountjoy). One can imagine the Crusader soldiers falling to the ground through sheer exhilaration at the sight of the city, giving prayers and exclaiming in excitement. For Richard the Lionheart, however, this was as far as he got in 1192, before having to turn back without being able to reach the city itself. The mosque situated on top of the mountain, has the remains of a church dating from Crusader times (1157), as well as the traditional tomb of the Hebrew prophet Samuel (1 Samuel 25:1). Recent excavations have brought to light significant remains from the Crusader period, including very large stables.

Decorated wall plaster from Mamila, showing the head of a saint or dignitary.

Crusader Jerusalem

The conquest of Jerusalem by the Franks during 15-18 July 1099 resulted in the rape and slaughter of its local inhabitants. A constant flow of blood ran in the streets for days on end. Such brutality and carnage had never been witnessed in the city before, or at least not in such a wanton fashion. The sparse population that survived was eventually banished and the Crusaders then began rebuilding the "ghost" city, with restoration and repopulation activities, and with the construction of churches, palaces, markets, inns and hospitals. The Church of the Holy Sepulcher, the place in which the Tomb of Jesus (the *Edicule*) was situated, was also quite substantially built and much of the façade of the church visible today dates from that time.

Top and center: the façade of the Church of the Holy Sepulcher, largely dating from the time of the Crusaders. *Bottom*: the modern Muristan quarter, originally a Crusader-period quarter adjacent to the Church of the Holy Sepulcher.

Ibn al-Athir: "The population of the holy city was put to the sword, and the Franj spent a week massacring Muslims. They killed more than seventy thousand in al-Aqsa Mosque"; Ibn al-Qalanisi: "Many people were killed. The Jews had gathered in their synagogue and the Franj burned them alive. They also destroyed monuments of saints and the tomb of Abraham, may peace be upon him!"

(A. Maalouf, The Crusades Through Arab Eyes, 1984, pp. 50-51).

The Church of the Holy Sepulcher and the Lutheran Church, after a fall of snow.

Jehan de Nueville (12th century): "There is grief in Jerusalem and grief in the land, where the Lord of His Goodness in suffering died... For whoso takes the Cross for God, pure though he be, when he but forsakes the Cross; then his God denies. So he, with Judas, be lost to Paradise."

(M. Grindea ed., Jerusalem: The Holy City in Literature, 1981, p. 161).

One of the two carved lintels from the doorways leading into the Church of the Holy Sepulcher, now in the Rockefeller Museum.

The Dormition Abbey
on Mount Zion.

Mount Zion and the Last Supper

The traditional spot of the Last Supper, where Jesus supped with his disciples before his arrest and subsequent crucifixion, is pointed out within a remarkable room with exquisite vaults dating from the Crusader-period located on Mount Zion, not far from the traditional Tomb of David. In archaeological terms, however, the room was clearly a side-chamber within the overall 12th century C.E. Church of St. Mary and there is absolutely no reason to situate the place of the meal in the Upper City. It seems more likely that Jesus spent his last meal in the area of the Lower City ("City of David"), south of the Temple Mount and close to the Spring of Siloam, from where he and his disciples would have had ease of access to the Mount of Olives and Gethsamene.

Top: the traditional Room of the Last Supper on Mount Zion. Bottom: the summit of Mount Zion to the northwest, with the Dormition Abbey (center, right) and the complex of the Tomb of David and the Room of the Last Supper.

"And he [Jesus] sent Peter and John, saying, Go and prepare the passover, that we may eat. And they said unto him, Where wilt thou that we prepare? And he said unto them, Behold, when ye are entered into the city, there shall a man meet you, bearing a pitcher of water; follow him into the house where he entereth in. And ye shall say unto the good-man of the house, The Master saith unto thee, Where is the guest chamber, where I shall eat the Passover with my disciples? And he shall shew you a large upper room furnished: there make ready." (Luke 22: 8-12).

"And it came to pass, while he [Jesus] blessed them, he was parted from them, and carried up into heaven." (Luke 24:51)

Mount of Olives and the Chapel of Ascension

There are numerous churches with archaeological remains dotting the landscape of the Mount of Olives and et-Tur. The octagonal Chapel of Christ's Ascension is one of the more interesting, since the surface of the rock shown inside is said to bear the footprint of Jesus himself. According to tradition, this chapel marks the spot where Jesus is said to have ascended to heaven. The chapel dates from the time of the Crusades but it may have been built on earlier Byzantine foundations. Entering the building, there is an oblong marble enclosure on the floor in which one is shown the impression of a right foot positioned towards the south. *Baedeker's Guide* of 1876 notes that "since the time of Frankish domination this footprint has been so variously described, that it must have been frequently renewed since then."

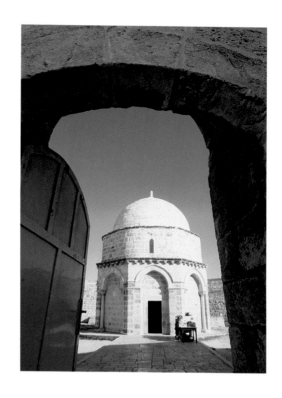

Bernardino Amico (late 16th century): "…on the pavement of the hard marble floor is impressed, as in wax, the print of our Saviour Jesus Christ, and these are the last vestiges he left on ascending into heaven… The other foot-print, according to hearsay, has been removed by the Muslims; and they keep it in their temple [Haram al-Sharif]".

Opposite page: the summit of the Mount of Olives.
Top and left: the Chapel of Ascension.

Crusaders along the Mediterranean Coast

Although the target of the Crusades was, of course, the Holy City of Jerusalem, which was conquered in 1099, many of their most important towns and forts were established along the coast of Palestine, at the time of the expansion of the Kingdom of Jerusalem during the reign of Baldwin I (1100-1118) and thereafter. Crusader remains have been uncovered at Acre (Akko), Athlit, Dor, Arsuf (Apollonia), Caesarea and Ascalon (Ashkelon), and at many other locations.

Acre (Akko)

Captured by the Crusaders in 1104, Acre was fortified and extensively built up. Much information about the appearance of the town has been obtained in recent archaeological excavations, combined with information derived from pilgrim's accounts and medieval maps.

A ceramic glazed vessel from the thirteenth century depicting a woman spinning yarn. *Opposite*: a ceramic glazed vessel depicting a soldier (*left*), and a stone carved heraldic device (*right*).

Wilibrand von Oldenburg (1212): "This is a fine and strong city situated on the seashore in such a way that, while it is quadrangular in shape, two of its sides forming an angle are girdled and protected by the sea; the other two are encompassed by a fine, wide and deep ditch, stone-lined to the very bottom, and by a double wall fortified with towers..."

(D. Jacoby, "Montmusard, Suburb of Crusader Acre", in B.Z. Kedar et al., eds., Outremer. Studies in the Crusading Kingdom of Jerusalem Presented to Joshua Prawer, 1982, p. 212)

The fortified Old City of Acre surrounding by stormy waves.

Ibn Jubair (1185): "Akkah [Acre] is the chief of the Frank cities of Syria, the great port of the sea, and the great anchorage for their ships, being second only to Constantinople. It is the meeting-place of Muslim and Christian merchants of all lands. The place is full of pigs and crosses."

(G. Le Strange, Palestine Under the Muslims, 1890, p. 174)

Top: the fortified walls of the fortress Athlit and (*bottom*) Athlit seen at dusk from the north. *Below*: a tombstone of a builder decorated with a large cross from Athlit.

Athlit

Although difficult to access owing to its present function as an Israeli navy post, the castle of Athlit is extremely impressive from the air. The castle (Chateau Pelerin) was built by the Templars between 1217 and 1218, and a town eventually grew up around it to the west. Archaeological excavations were undertaken at the time of the British Mandate, uncovering the fortifications, the town and a burial ground with numerous tombstones.

The Athlit cemetery in 2004: "The southwestern corner [of the cemetery] is being eroded by the Mediterranean Sea, resulting in the exposure of a burial. The tombstones themselves show significant erosion since they were uncovered in 1934."

(J. A. Thompson, Bulletin of the Anglo-Israel Archaeological Society 22, 2004, p. 97)

Arsuf (Apollonia)

Athlit •

Arsuf •

Arsuf fell to the Crusaders in 1101 and was taken with the aid of the Genoese fleet. In recent years the impressive castle of Arsuf has been exposed during archaeological excavations conducted at the site. It had massive walls with semi-circular and square towers and was surrounded by a moat. In 1265 the final defense of the town took place and following the collapse of parts of the walls by the Baybars the town surrendered.

Top and bottom: two views of the fortified castle of Arsuf. *Top, left*: a glazed ceramic vessel depicting a griffin from Dor/Tantura (Merle).

Following the success at Arsuf in 1191, Richard the Lionheart (Malik al-Inkitar) prevailed upon al-'Adil to come to an agreement: "Men of ours and of yours have died, the country is in ruins, and events have entirely escaped anyone's control. Do you not believe that it is enough? As far as we are concerned, there are only three subjects of discord: Jerusalem, the True Cross, and territory."

(A. Maalouf, The Crusades Through Arab Eyes, 1984, p. 211).

Caesarea

Between the time of the Frankish conquest of Caesarea in 1101 and the dismantling of the defenses of the city by al-Ashraf Khalil in 1291, the city walls were rebuilt and razed on many different occasions. Major refortification works were undertaken by John of Brienne in 1217 and by Louis IX in 1251. Excavated in the early 1960s by archaeologists, Caesarea has the best preserved town fortification walls in the country, notwithstanding the destruction to them wrought by al-Ashraf Khalil.

William of Tyre speaking about the 1101 massacre of the Muslim inhabitants of Caesarea by the Crusaders, indicated that it was so terrible an event "that the feet of the destroyers were stained with the blood of the slain."

Ascalon (Ashkelon)

Conquering Ascalon was quite a complicated feat for the Crusaders in 1153. They were forced to mount a two-month siege of the walled Muslim town using battering rams and siege-towers built out of wood taken from dismantled ships. The Crusader fortifications formed a semi-circle around the town, and segments of it are still visible today. There was also a large church of St. John, but its whereabouts is still unknown. Recent excavations brought to light a Fatimid inscribed plaque which was later used in the 13th century to depict the arms of Sir Hugh Wake of County Lincoln who took part in the rebuilding of the defenses of Ascalon.

Center: a view of the Crusader fortifications at Caesarea. *Top and left*: a gold bracelet and two medieval glazed vessels from Caesarea. *Bottom*: a Fatimid Arabic inscription from Ascalon with superimposed Crusader heraldic devices over it.

Painted on a light blue background on the vault of a church in Ascalon, a pious invocation: "O Morning Star, Protectress of sailors. Pray for us!"

(D. Pringle, The Churches of the Crusader Kingdom of Jerusalem, Vol. 1, 1993, p. 67)

The ruined walls of
Crusader Ascalon.

Crusader Churches

A recent survey of churches that were built by the Crusaders in the Holy Land in the 12th and 13 centuries has shown that out of some 400 identified from the written sources, at least half of these have survived only as archaeological ruins or as structural remnants incorporated into later buildings and even within mosques. The most important of these was the Church of the Holy Sepulcher in Jerusalem which was also the seat of the patriarch, but other churches of significance existed throughout the country, notably at Caesarea, Nazareth, Hebron, Sebastia, and Lydda, but many more existed within small towns and villages.

Top and opposite: two views of the summit of Mount Tabor. *Bottom*: the interior of the church on Mount Tabor.

"The architects, artists and artisans responsible for building churches in the Crusader kingdom in the twelfth and thirteenth centuries included both easterners and westerners. The stylistic influences to be detected in them are therefore diverse. However, a great deal more painstaking documentation of existing structures will need to be done before any general assessment can be made about the respective architectural contributions of East to West, and of West to East, at the time of the Crusades." (D. Pringle, "Church-Building in the Kingdom of Jerusalem," Bulletin of the Anglo-Israel Archaeological Society, 14, 1994-95, p. 77).

Mount Tabor

Various Benedictine establishments also had churches, notably the monastery situated on the summit of Mount Tabor. This was the place where tradition placed the transfiguration of Jesus (Matthew 17: 1-8).

Mount Tabor: "The perfect breast shape of Mount Tabor excites awe and wonder; it has the aura of a sacred mountain. From the dawn of history it was a place where humanity found contact with the unknown..." (J. Murphy O'Connor, The Holy Land, 1992, p. 369)

Nahal Siyah

The Carmelites, an order of Latin hermits, built between *c.* 1220 and 1283 a church and monastery of St. Mary in Nahal Siyah on the western side of Mount Carmel near Haifa. A cave associated with the prophet Elijah existed in the vicinity of the Carmelite monastery.

A French pilgrimage text from c. 1231: "…on the edge of the same mountain there is a very beautiful and delightful place, where there live the Latin hermits who are called the Brothers of the Carmel (freres du Carme) and where there is a small church of Our Lady; and throughout this place there is a great profusion of good waters which issue from the very rock of the mountain."

(quoted in D. Pringle, The Churches of the Crusader Kingdom of Jerusalem, Volume II, p. 249).

Top left and bottom: two views of the chapel in Nahal Siyah. *Top right*: the ruined church at the traditional location of Jacob's Well.

Jacob's Well

An interesting Crusader Church of the Savior is preserved at the traditional site of Jacob's Well at the foot of Mount Gerizim close to Nablus. The church and the village lands of Balata belonged to the Benedictine nuns of Bethany. The church was cleared and restored by the Greek Orthodox Patriarchate in the nineteenth century, but the church was never completely rebuilt.

Nahal Siyah •

Jacob's Well •

Theodoric (c. 1175): "The well… is half a mile distant from the city [Nablus]: it lies in front of the altar in the church built over it, in which nuns devote themselves to the service of God. This well is called the Fountain of Jacob…"

Crusader Fortresses

There are almost one hundred fortresses of various types (solitary towers to hilltop castles) within the Crusader territory of the Kingdom of Jerusalem. Such fortresses have massive fortifications, towers, massive gates, posterns and moats. The ramparts are built of large and well dressed ashlars and embossed blocks of stone. Beneath the fortresses are large water storage facilities. Single towers have been found at various sites, such as at Jaba', Ka'akun and Burj el-Ahmar (the Red Tower).

A carved helmeted head of a soldier from the Monfort excavations.

The excavators found the "workshop of the castle in which armor was repaired. Here were found blooms of iron, a crucible, various tools, hammers, chisels, fragments of chain-mail, pieces of a basinet, a bit of the visor of a great helm (would that we had more of it – it is unique!), scales of body defenses (jazerans), upward of forty bits of armor. Here also were heads of arrows, darts, lances, spikes, all lying in a bed of charcoal, indicating that they had remained there since the burning of the castle."

(B. Dean, A Crusader's Fortress in Palestine, 1927, p. 22)

Montfort

Montfort is a remarkable fortress situated above a deep gorge with a tangled grove of evergreen trees in the western Galilee. Built in 1226 or 1227, the fortress eventually became the headquarters of the Teutonic Order who enlarged it considerably. It was eventually captured by Baybars in 1271 when part of the southern wall was undermined by his troops; this led to the surrender of the knights. Archaeological excavations were conducted at the site in 1926, revealing parts of the fortress that had been hidden beneath the rubble, as well as enormous quantities of artifacts. A remarkable helmeted head of a sculpture was uncovered in the area of the chapel.

223

Top and bottom: oblique and bird's eye views of the castle of Belvoir.

Belvoir

Belvoir

Belmont

Unlike Montfort, which had very little strategic value, Belvoir (Kokhav ha-Yarden), situated in the Jordan Valley to the north of Beth Shean, was situated at a spot where it could guard a number of major highways leading in different directions. Indeed the view from the fortress is quite spectacular. Acquired by the Hospitallers in 1168, the castle was characterized by double-enclosure fortifications which made it difficult to conquer. However, Salah-ed-Din managed to conquer the fortress in 1189 following his successful battle at the Horns of Hattin, and it was apparently garrisoned by soldiers at least until 1219 when it was finally destroyed. Most of the fortress was exposed during archaeological excavations at the site in the 1960's.

Top and bottom: two views of the castle of Belmont surrounded by the houses of the Ottoman village of Suba.

James Finn, the British Consul, who visited the village of Suba in 1858: "In the village we found remains of old masonry, most likely the basement of a fortification of early Saracenic or the Crusader's era; besides which there was a piece of wall in excellent condition…" (J. Finn, Byeways in Palestine, 1868, p. 426).

A carving from Belvoir of a winged angel holding a book.

Belmont

Beneath the ruins of the abandoned Arab village of Suba, next to the present-day Kibbutz Tsuba, west of Jerusalem, are the prominent remains of the Hospitaller castle of Belmont. Existing by 1171-72, the castle eventually fell to Salah-ed-Din in 1187 and was destroyed in 1191. Excavations have revealed substantial remains of the fortifications of the castle, as well as its inner ward with vaulted ranges around a courtyard with a well-built wine press in one corner. The church was probably situated beneath the remains of the late Ottoman mosque near the summit of the hill.

A general view of Kala'at Jiddin. *Right*: the fortifications of Burj el-Ahmar (*top*) and Ka'akun (*bottom*).

Kala'at Jiddin

Much of what can be seen of the old masonry in the heart of Kala'at Jiddin is from the 18th century, but deep within the tumble and debris are wall fragments and tell-tale signs of Crusader masonry. These are remnants of the castle (Iudin) built by the Teutonic order in the1220s or 1230s which is similar in layout to Rhineland castles.

Ka'akun and Burj el-Ahmar

Fortified towers which once stood to a height of two or three stories, have been found at various sites throughout the country. Ka'akun was already in existence as a defensive tower in 1123. Burj el-Ahmar (the "Red Tower") has been excavated and the results indicate that it was built in c. 1110 and destroyed by the Mamluks in 1265.

Burchard of Mount Sion (c. 1283):
"…four leagues from Acre, in the mountains of Saron, is a castle called Iudin, which belonged to the Teutonic House but is now destroyed."

A general view of the site of Mezad Ateret. Note the excavated section of wall in the foreground.

Vadum Jacob (Mezad Ateret)

Vadum Jacob
Safed

This castle of the Templars (Le Chastelet) is situated on an ancient mound at the southern end of the Hula Valley, close to the Bridge of Jacob's Daughters (hence the name Vadum Jacob, meaning "Jacob's Ford"). It was built in October 1178 and the manpower that was used for the construction work consisted of the entire Frankish army provided by Baldwin IV. Salah-ed-Din (Saladin) attacked the site in August 1179, and excavations have shown that the Muslims attacked from three directions, setting fire to the doors of the castle and firing large numbers of arrowheads at the defenders. Eventually the castle fell and its inhabitants were slaughtered.

Iron work-tools discovered during excavations at the site.

"At the time when Saladin attacked, construction was at its height and the castle consisted of half-finished walls and incomplete vaults probably with scaffolding in place, temporary walls, iron tools scattered about, piles of mortar and lime, dressed stones and earthen ramps. Around the exterior and interior of the walls were plastered tracks intended for the carts hauled by oxen which carried stones from the quarry…" (A. Boas, Crusader Archaeology, 1999, p. 119).

Safed (Zefat)

At the top of an oval hill within the modern town of Zefat are the remains of a medieval fortress with round towers. Historical sources indicate that the castle was built in 1102, refortified by King Fulk (c. 1138-40) and went through various stages of rebuilding before it was destroyed by the Ayyubids in 1218-1219. The fortress was rebuilt by the Templars in 1240 and by Baybars who captured the place in 1266. Hardly anything was known about the architecture of this fortress until recent excavations uncovered parts of the Crusader ramparts and a tower-gate complex. Within the rubble archaeologists found a battered sculpted head of 12th century date.

A general view of one of the streets of the old city of Safed today

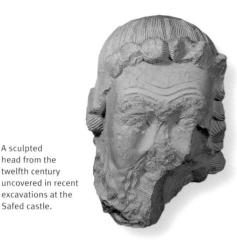

A sculpted head from the twelfth century uncovered in recent excavations at the Safed castle.

Text from c. 1260-66: "Among the other excellent features which the castle of Saphet has, it is notable that it can be defended by a few and that many can gather under the protection of its walls and it cannot be besieged except by a very great multitude; but such a multitude would not have supplies for very long since it would find neither water nor food, nor can a very great multitude be near at the same time and, if they are scattered in remote places, they cannot help one another. You cannot realize how useful and necessary the castle is to the whole of the Christian lands..." (translation in H. Kennedy, Crusader Castles, 1995, p. 197)

The castle of Safed on the summit of the town.

Crusader Agriculture

On the basis of the writings of Ibn Jabayr one would have to conclude that agricultural activities in the Kingdom of Jerusalem were solely in the hands of the local Muslim population, even though the supervision of this agricultural work was undertaken by the Franks. Archaeology, however, has shown that this was not the case. Indeed, agricultural estates and farm buildings have been studied in different parts of the country. To the east of the castle of Monfort is an isolated tower known as Burj Misr (Mezad Abirim) built of large ashlar blocks. It appears to have been used as a fortified farmhouse in the 12th century. Large rural estates are also known. Some of these estates, such as at Jaba' near Ramallah, have fortified towers, stables and open reservoirs. At the rural estate at Khirbet Iqbala / En Hemed (Aqua Bella), not far from Suba, a large building was used as an infirmary for the Order of St. John. Oil presses, wine presses, and sugar mills have been found at a number of sites.

Above: the fortified farm-house at Mezad Abirim. *Opposite*: The agricultural estate at Aqua Bella west of Jerusalem.

Ibn Jubayr: "…we passed through an unbroken skein of farms and villages whose lands were efficiently cultivated. The inhabitants were all Muslims, but they live with comfort with the Franj – may God preserve us from temptation! Their dwellings belong to them and all their property is unmolested. All the regions controlled by the Franj in Syria are subject to this same system: the landed domains, villages and farms have remained in the hands of the Muslims." (A. Maalouf, The Crusades Through Arab Eyes, 1984, p. 263).

The Horns of Hattin

The Battle of Hattin was very decisive and changed the course of events like no other battle before between the Crusaders and the Muslims. Salah-ed-Din (Saladin) organized his troops and waited for the Crusaders. He needed a clear-cut and decisive victory. Towards noon on the 4 July 1187 a very tired and thirsty Frankish army arrived at the site of a promontory known as the "Horns of Hattin", situated above a village of the same name, with the glittering Sea of Galilee in the distance. The exhausted soldiers wanted to reach the lake to slake their thirst, but decided to do so after engaging the Muslims in battle. During the subsequent battle one of their commanders, Count Raymond of Tripoli, fled the scene, leaving his soldiers to their fate. The Crusaders fought with all their might and then retreated to the upper part of the hill. This was where the final stage of the battle was fought; eventually the Crusaders capitulated and the leading prisoners, King Guy and Prince Arnat, were brought before the victorious Salah-ed-Din. In the following days and weeks Salah-ed-Din managed to conquer most of the important towns and strongholds that were once in the possession of the Crusaders.

Thus, under the difficult circumstances of the final battle, the ascent to the horns made considerable military sense: the ancient walls provided some protection from Muslim arrows and allowed the Frankish archers to shoot at their enemies as if from the ramparts of a castle. It is likely that the Frankish knights regrouped in the large crater between the horns..."

(B.Z. Kedar, ed., The Horns of Hattin, 1992, p. 206)

Top, left and *right*: three views of the battlefield at the Horns of Hattin.

According to Ibn al-Athir: "The Muslims had set fire to the dry grass, and the wind was blowing the smoke into the eyes of the knights. Assailed by thirst, flames and smoke, by the summer heat and the fires of combat, the Franj were unable to go on. But they believed they could avoid death only by confronting it. They launched attacks so violent that the Muslims were about to give way. Nevertheless, with each assault the Franj suffered heavy losses and their numbers diminished. The Muslims gained possession of the [relics of the] True Cross. For the Franj, this was the heaviest of losses, for it was on this cross, they claim, that the Messiah, peace be upon him, was crucified."

(A. Maalouf, The Crusades Through Arab Eyes, 1984, p.192).

Kala'at Nimrud

Kala'at Nimrud (or Subayba) is the largest medieval fortress in Israel, but it was not built by the Crusaders. The man behind the building project was al-'Aziz 'Uthman, the Ayyubid governor of nearby Banias, and construction took place between 1228 and 1230. The entire fortress was rebuilt by the Mamluks at the time of the Sultan Baybars.

Below and *opposite*: three views of the fortifications and gate of the castle of Kala'at Nimrud.

A monumental Arabic inscription from the site dating from the reign of Sultan Baybars reads: "In the name of God, the Merciful, the Compassionate. This blessed tower was renewed by the grace of our lord, the Sultan al-Malik al-Zahir, the most splendid master, the scholar, the just, the fighter of the holy war, the warrior on the border, the heavenly assisted, the victorious..."
(M. Hartal, The Al-Subayba (Nimrod) Fortress, 2001, p. 110).

Burj al-Malih

On the eastern edges of the hills of Samaria, overlooking the Jordan Valley, is an interesting fortified site containing a gate and a number of buildings of Crusader or Mamluke date. It was first mapped by the explorers C.R. Conder and H.H. Kitchener in 1874, but modern archaeological work has not yet been conducted at the site.

The fortified enclosure of Burj el-Malih.

Caravanserai in the Galilee

Caravanserai (*khans*) appear at numerous sites dating from the 14th to 19th centuries. They served to facilitate the traffic of pilgrims and merchant caravans along major roads, providing room and board and stabling. The earlier *khans* known from the Galilee – Khan Jubb Yusuf (14th century) and Khan el-Tujjar (15th/16th century) – were apparently built at the behest of Mamluk officials and were fortified. Khan Jubb Yusuf was built on the line of the *Via Maris*, a major trade route linking Syria with Jerusalem and the south. The khan derives its name from the belief held by certain Arab geographers that it was here that Joseph was thrown into a pit by his brethren (Genesis 37: 17-29). The site of the pit is situated beneath a small domed structure next to the khan. In 1877 Conder and Kitchener visited the khan and declared that it was "still in very good repair". This is no longer the case.

The domed structure above the traditional "Pit of Joseph" at Khan Jubb Yusuf.

The later caravanserai at Khan Gaaton.

Top: a caravanserai situated at Kefar Harib, next to the road leading to the Golan Heights. *Bottom*: a general view of the caravanserai buildings at Khan Jubb Yusuf.

Part Six:

TOWARDS MODERN TIMES
Ottoman Palestine

Palestine flourished in the early Ottoman period. The important towns of this period were Jerusalem, Tabariya (Tiberias), Nablus (Shechem), Khalil (Hebron) and Akkah (Acre). Western pilgrimage was encouraged and Christian visitors stayed at caravanserai, built next to highways and within towns. Numerous villages sprang up in different parts of the country and their houses eventually became the core structural components of present-day Arab villages. Dahr el-Umar, a local chieftain, fortified the towns of Acre and Tiberias, and built forts at Shefar'am, and Sasa, among other places. The country was administered by pashas and as time passed the taxes on the local population became more and more burdensome. Ottoman rule ceased with the arrival of the British in 1917.

A stone head made in the nineteenth century and sold
in Moses Shapira's antiquities shop in Jerusalem

The Walls of Jerusalem

The wonderful Old City walls of Jerusalem that we see today were the brainchild of the Ottoman ruler Sulayman the Magnificent and were planned and executed by his master court architect (Hassa Mi'mar) and administrative genius Sinan in the 1540s. Strange as it may seem, none of them ever got to visit Jerusalem and so they never ever managed to see the results. The wall surrounding Jerusalem is pierced by many gates and inscriptions commemorating the construction works appear above the gates. Just inside Jaffa Gate, tourist guides like pointing out the tombs of the "engineers" who forgot to include Mount Zion within the city walls and so for their forgetfulness were beheaded. This is actually a fable and the tombs are of certain holy Muslims.

Top: Damascus Gate and the northern Old City wall built at the time of Sulayman the Magnificent, towards the south. Note in the distance the gold dome of the Dome of the Rock, marking the Haram al-Sharif (Temple Mount), and the slopes of Mount of Olives to the far left. *Left*: a window in the Zion Gate bearing the pock-marked signs of the battle over the city in 1967.

Sulayman was clearly not a modest man and this is how he described himself in 1521: "King of kings, sovereign of sovereigns, most high Emperor of Byzantium and Trebizond, all powerful King of Persia, Arabia, Syria and Egypt, Supreme Lord of Europe and Asia, Prince of Mecca and Aleppo, Master of Jerusalem, and Ruler of the Universal Sea…" (A. Bridge, Suleiman the Magnificent, 1983, p. 55).

Three gates in the Old City wall: the blocked Golden Gate (*left*), the Zion Gate (*center*), and the Dung Gate (*right*).

Mosques

The earliest mosques (from the Arabic *masjid*, "a place of prostrations") found in the Holy Land extend back to the Umayyad period. Some of the earliest mosques are open-air shrines uncovered at sites in the Negev Desert. The most important mosque in the country is the Aqsa Mosque on the Haram al-Sharif in Jerusalem. A semi-circular niche called the *mihrab*, indicates the direction of prayer towards Mecca (*qiblah*). Next to the *mihrab* is the pulpit (*minbar*) from where the Friday sermon is delivered. Many mosques were built in the country during the Ottoman period. Religious shrines (known as *maqam*, meaning "sacred place") associated with local Muslim saints are also scattered throughout the countryside, and next to them occasionally are ancient holy trees.

Top: mosque at Sidni Ali. *Bottom left*: mosque at Yavne. *Bottom right*: the Neby Musa procession in an engraving from 1881.

"As soon as they are in sight of the shrine of the Prophet they rearrange the group, unfurl the banner and begin the formal procession again. First they raise small heaps of stones as qanatir ["witnesses"], and recite the fatihah. The dervish who heads the procession sends one of his followers to announce their coming to the other dervishes who are already in Nebi Musa.."

(T. Canaan, Mohammedan Saints and Sanctuaries, 1927, p.199)

The Muslim pilgrimage center at Neby Musa.

Neby Musa

Once a year thousands of Muslims descend from Jerusalem in procession to Neby Musa, in the desert not far to the north-west of the Dead Sea, where they spend five days praying and feasting. The place is where, according to tradition, Moses was venerated by pilgrims on their way to Mecca. A shrine was built at this location by the Mamluk Sultan Baybars in 1269, but most of the buildings visible today were constructed during the Ottoman period.

A tale told by a Muslim from Abu Dis: "When the shepherd had lived out his days he swooned away, and his friends, supposing him dead, buried him in the place where his grave is still shown, not far from the shrine of Neby Musa. But he is not dead, for in consequence of Musa's words, 'May you never die', he cannot find rest in death, but is still alive and wanders about pasturing the ibex… He has been seen in the act of casting himself off a precipitous cliff, attempting suicide in his despair; but in vain. He is described as a very tall old man, covered with white hair, his beard and nails exceedingly long. He always takes flight if one tries to approach him."

(J. E. Hanauer, Folk-Lore of the Holy Land, 1907, p. 38).

243

Tiberias

Quite a few towns and villages in the Galilee rose to prominence under the rule of the local chieftain Daher el-Umar in the mid-eighteenth century, resulting is the construction of fortresses at Sasa, Dayr Hanna, Jiddin, Tel Harbaj, and Saffuriya (Sepphoris), and major fortifications at Acre, Haifa, Nazareth and Tiberias. In many instances the new walls were built over much earlier Crusader and Mamluk fortifications.

"…On his return from Mecca, Sulayman [Ottoman Vali of Damascus] was once again ordered to take up the cudgels against Dahir, and this time he was provided with even greater reinforcements than he had been on the previous occasion. Siege experts, together with a whole shipload of special equipment, were landed at Haifa from whence they were to proceed to Tiberias. Separate firmans were sent to the Vali of Tripoli and to the zu 'ama and timariots of Damascus, ordering them to come to Sulayman's aid. And so, the latter once again set off for Tiberias, this time determined finally to put an end to Dahir. But, as fate would have it, he died suddenly on the way (at the end of August 1743) and the campaign was called off." (A. Cohen, Palestine in the 18th century, 1973, p. 35).

Opposite, top and center: mid-eighteenth century fortifications of Tiberias built by Daher el-Umar.

Shefar'am

Shefar'am is the site of a fortress which was apparently built by 'Uthman son of Daher el-Umar in 1768/69 on top of earlier Crusader remains. This is confirmed by an inscription that was once seen over the gate. Within the fortress are seven enormous vaulted chambers.

Fortress from the time of Daher el-Umar at Shefar'am.

Inscription over the gate:
"Stop at a house in which charity manifested themselves increasingly. It was constructed by the generous 'Othman who was given to be a lord. His house is the full moon upon which the lion sat. It was habitually frequented by guests. Look at the chronogram; verily this is the abode of happiness."

(A Petersen, "The Fortress of Shafr'Amr and Related Buildings," Levant 32, 2000, p. 92).

Acre

The city of Acre is situated over and against one of the most important harbors along the eastern littoral of the Mediterranean Sea. It is not surprising, therefore, than many countries and armies have fought over it at different points in time with bitterness and desperation, with the result that many soldiers lost their lives in its defense or while attacking it. Today, the Old City is a tourist attraction and visitors wander around the markets, visit the underground Crusader parts and gape at the beauty of its battlements and mosques.

Crusader Akko was rebuilt at the time of the local chieftain Daher el-Umar in the mid-eighteenth century, and the fortifications and many of its buildings were restored by his successor, of Albanian origin, Ahmad Pasha, known as el-Jazzar ("the butcher"). With the support of the British fleet, el-Jazzar was able to defend an offensive by Napoleon Bonaparte in 1799. The siege lasted 60 days and was a disaster all around.

Top: Acre and its eighteenth-century fortifications, with the Mediterranean Sea in the background. *Bottom*: the impressive mosque of el-Jazzar (*left* and *right*)

"*The same fate befell al-Jazzar's men, whose unburied bodies served as prey to hordes of stray dogs. An exception was Major Thomas Oldfield, a British Naval officer killed on 7 May and retrieved from the battlefield by the French due to a misidentification. He was laid to rest by the French with full military honors…*"

(A. Berman, "Excavation of the Courthouse Site at 'Akko: A Siege-Trench of Bonarparte's Army…," 'Atiqot 31, 1997, p. 92)

Top and bottom: three views of Sulayman Pasha's aqueduct to Acre.

The Aqueduct to Acre

The Acre aqueduct ("Kinat el-Basha"), built on a series of arches, is seen next to the road to Nahariya north of Acre (Akko). It is an extremely impressive example of hydraulic architecture, even though bits of it occasionally collapse after the winter rains. It was built by Sulayman Pasha in 1815 to supply Acre with water, and replaced another on a slightly different line which was built by el-Jazzar and destroyed by Napoleon Bonaparte during his siege of Acre. Sulayman Pasha had command over the construction of the aqueduct himself, making sure that measurements were taken to determine the best route, and getting local villagers to supply quicklime for plastering the channel of the aqueduct. It took one year to build. Three and a half hours was the time it took for water to reach Acre from the point of origin (the spring of ʿAin Basha).

"According to his [Sulayman Pasha's] biographer El Aura, the Pasha himself supervised the work over a period of many months. Thus in the main the present aqueduct would be [in 1946] about 130 years old. Suleiman's successor ʿAbdullah Pasha is said to have used the water to irrigate his various farms between Umm el-Faraj and El-Bahja, to the north of the Stock farm; and at El-Bahja his reservoir is still in use on the property of the Beydoun family."

(N. Makhouly and C.N. Johns, Guide to Acre, 1946, p. 94).

Abu Ghosh

The real name of the village is Kiryat el-Enab (Arabic for "Village of the Grapes") but today everyone knows it as Abu Ghosh, the place west of Jerusalem where one can eat some of the best food around (especially *hummous*, made of crushed chickpeas). Few know that it is derived from the name of a bandit, Issa Mohammed Abu Ghosh, a Bedouin hailing from the Hedjaz, who levied an exorbitant toll on travelers passing along the Jaffa-Jerusalem road in the late eighteenth and early nineteenth centuries. If one did not comply with his demands one was thrown into a dungeon, or worse. Recent archaeological excavations have brought to light substantial remains of the Ottoman houses from that period next to the principal mosque in the village.

Left: mosque in the village. *Right*: trees and garden in front of the Church of Kiryat el-Enab at Abu Ghosh.

The refectory in the Crusader church in the valley next to the village: "From about 1756 till 1834 it was used as a prison by the Sheikhs of Abu Ghosh. Many Franciscans taken on their way to Jerusalem, were imprisoned there until ransom was paid. The demand notes can be seen in the Franciscan Convent in Jerusalem." (E. Hoade, Guide to the Holy Land, 1973, p. 730)

1586 engraving of the Ottoman village of Abu Ghosh (*left*) and the recent excavations of Ottoman houses next to the village mosque (*right*).

The harbor of Jaffa, where the steamships arrived
from the west bringing pilgrims and travelers.

From Jaffa to Jaffa Gate: Stepping from Antiquity into Modern Times

The Jaffa Gate in Jerusalem, which was usually the first main port of call for travelers on reaching the Holy Land.

Travelers and pilgrims reaching Palestine by steamship in the nineteenth century disembarked at the port of Jaffa and made their way by carriage towards Jerusalem, with the lofty intention of seeing its holy sites and antiquities. But in practical terms the first thing they usually wanted to do on reaching the Jaffa Gate was to find an appropriate hotel or hostel where they could get a good meal and a comfortable bed. Jerusalem was an exhilarating city for many, and a disappointment for a few, but everybody found something that they could comment upon. The Jaffa Road of 1867, in the photography by Corporal Henry Phillips, was an empty landscape with only the Russian Compound looming in the distance; today, Jaffa Road in the center of town is now completely built-up, with numerous shops, and with a constant flow of traffic. As in many parts of the city, archaeological excavations were also undertaken in the area beneath the plaza in front of the Jaffa Gate before construction began, revealing interesting caves from the Iron Age, a Byzantine street and a bath-house, and other remains from medieval times.

Index of Places Mentioned in Book

Select List of Publications

Aerial Photography

* Arden-Close, C. 1941. "Sir Aurel Stein's Explorations of the Roman Frontiers in Iraq and Transjordan", *Palestine Exploration Fund Quarterly Statement* 73: 18-21.
* Cleave, R. 1993. *The Holy Land: A Unique Perspective*. Oxford.
* Dalman, G. 1925. *Hundert deutsche Fliegerbilder aus Palästina*. Gütersloh.
* Deuel, L., 1969. *Flights into Yesterday: The Story of Aerial Photography*. Harmondsworth.
* Gavish, D. 1978. "Air-photographs by First World War Pilots in Eretz Israel," *Cathedra* 7: 119-150 (Hebrew).
* Gavish, D. 1990. "Aerial Perspective of Past Landscapes". Pp. 308-319 in R. Kark (ed.), *The Land That Became Israel: Studies in Historical Geography*. New Haven.
* Kedar, B. Z. 1999. *The Changing Land: Between the Jordan and the Sea. Aerial Photographs from 1917 to the Present*. Jerusalem.
* Kedar, B. Z. and Danin, A., (ed.) 2000. *Remote Sensing: The Use of Aerial Photographs and Satellite Images in Israel Studies*. Jerusalem.
* Kennedy, D. L., 1989. *Into the Sun: Essays in Air Photography in Archaeology in Honour of Derrick Riley*. Sheffield.
* Kennedy, D. L. and Bewley, R. 2004. *Ancient Jordan from the Air*. Oxford.
* Kennedy, D. L. and Riley, D. N. 1990. *Rome's Desert Frontier from the Air*. London.
* Mouterde, R. and Poidebard, A. 1945. *Le Limes de Chalcis*. Paris.
* Pixler, Y. 1992. "The Use of Aerial Photographs for Locating Ancient Fields in the Region of Lod". Pp. 60-76 in S. Dar (ed.), *New Vistas in the Research of Ancient Agriculture and Economy of Eretz Israel*. Bar Ilan University.
* Poidebard, A. 1934. *Le Trace de Rome dans le desert de Syrie. Le Limes de Trajan à la conquete arabe. Recherches aériennes 1925-1932*. 2 vols. Paris.
* Riley, D. N., 1980. *Early Landscape from the Air*. Sheffield.
* Taylor, J. 1989. *High Above Jordan*. London.
* Taylor, J. 2005. *Jordan: Images from the Air*. Amman.
* Thomas, H. H. 1920."Geographical Reconnaissance by Aeroplane Photography with Special Reference to the Work Done on the Palestine Front," *Geographical Journal* LV: 249-376.
* Wiegand, T. 1920. *Sinai*. Berlin.
* Wilson, D.R. 1982. *Air Photo Interpretation For Archaeologists*. London.

Archaeology

* Aharoni, Y. 1982. *The Archaeology of the Land of Israel*. London.
* Bartlett, J.R. (ed.) 1997. *Archaeology and Biblical Interpretation*. London.
* Ben-Tor, A. (ed.) 1992. *The Archaeology of Ancient Israel*. New Haven.
* Levy, T.E. (ed.) 1995. *The Archaeology of Society in the Holy Land*. London.
* Mazar, A. 1990. *Archaeology of the Land of the Bible, 10,000-586 B.C.E.* New York.
* Murphy-O'Connor, J. 1992. *The Holy Land: An Archaeological Guide From Earliest Times to 1700*. Oxford.
* Negev, A. and Gibson, S. (eds.) 2001. *Archaeological Encyclopedia of the Holy Land*. New York.
* Rast, W.E., 1992. *Through the Ages in Palestinian Archaeology: An Introductory Handbook*. Philadelphia.
* Stern, E. (ed.), *The New Encyclopedia of Archaeological Excavations in the Holy Land*. 5 vols. (1993-2007). Jerusalem.

Acknowledgments

We would like to extend our thanks to the many people who helped during the production of this book.

First of all, to the many excavating archaeologists and photographers – too many to be named – who provided pictures and information about their sites. Secondly we are grateful to the various individuals from the Israel Antiquities Authority who supported this project from the outset, namely Shuka Dorfman, Director-General of the IAA; Dr Uzi Dahari, Assistant-Director; Dr Hava Katz, Director of the National Treasures Department; Pnina Shur and Yael Barschak of the Finds and Photographic Archives Department, and to Alon De Groot of the Scientific Reports Unit who prepared the initial list of sites.

We also wish to thank Dr Sam Wolff for his excellent editorial comments, to Rafi Lewis and Mareike Grosser for background research, to Yosh Gafni and Rachel Gilon for their advice, to Amalya Keshet from the Israel Museum and to Fauzi Ibrahim from the Rockfeller Museum for their assistance in co-ordinating photo shoots at these locations, to Dr John Hall for the satellite image, and to Dr Amnon Kartin for providing us with maps.

Aerial photographs and images taken on the ground in this book are copyrighted to Albatross. The Israel Antiquities Authority holds the copyright for the artifact images. Additional pictures were provided by Shimon Gibson who holds their copyright. In regard to additional unacknowledged pictures we have attempted to establish contact with copyright holders, but in some cases this was not possible. Should a copyright not have been acknowledged, we would be grateful if the publishers are contacted so that a correct acknowledgement may be made.

To all those who enjoy the study of the ancient landscapes of the land of Israel, this book is dedicated.

Duby Tal and Shimon Gibson

A view of the Kishon River glinting in the sun. A battle took place on the banks of this river between the northern tribes of Israel and the kings of Canaan, and was described poetically in the Song of Deborah: "The kings came and fought... They fought from heaven; the stars in their courses fought against Sisera. The river of Kishon swept them away, that ancient river, the river Kishon. O my soul, thou hast trodden down strength..." (Judges 5: 19-21).